GREAT BEGINNINGS

GREAT BEGINNINGS

OPENING LINES
OF GREAT
NOVELS

GEORGIANNE ENSIGN

HarperCollins*Publishers*

Copyright acknowledgments follow page 244.

GREAT BEGINNINGS. Copyright © 1993 by Georgianne Ensign. All rights reserved.
Printed in the United States of America. No part of this book may be used or repro-
duced in any manner whatsoever without written permission except in the case of brief
quotations embodied in critical articles and reviews. For information address Harper-
Collins Publishers, Inc., 10 East 53rd Street, New York, NY 10022.

HarperCollins books may be purchased for educational, business, or sales promotional
use. For information please write: Special Markets Department, HarperCollins Publishers, Inc., 10 East 53rd Street, New York, NY 10022.

FIRST EDITION

Designed by Jessica Shatan

Library of Congress Cataloging-in-Publication Data
Ensign, Georgianne, 1940–
   Great beginnings : opening lines of great novels / Georgianne Ensign.—1st ed.
     p. cm.
  ISBN 0-06-018331-4
   1. Fiction—Technique. 2. Openings (Rhetoric). 3. Quotations, English. I. Title.
PN3365.E57 1993
808.3—dc20   92-53367

93 94 95 96 97 ❖/RRD 10 9 8 7 6 5 4 3 2 1

To Julian Bach

Contents ∽

Acknowledgments

The idea for Great Beginnings occurred to me when my agent, Julian Bach, having been handed a manuscript of mine—an Edwardian love story—declared (somewhat jokingly) that the first test he applied to a novel was its beginning sentence. This passing comment made me curious about the beginnings of the great classics of Literature, and the search rapidly grew into this book, for which I thank him.

For their generous assistance in my research and in making possible the use of original holograph material, I am indebted to Michael Asquith, Professor Quentin Bell and Joseph Heller; Dr. Charles Cutter (Brandeis University Library), David C. Devenish (Wisbech and Fenland Museum), Charles E. Greene and Don C. Skemer (Princeton University Libraries), Francis O. Mattson (Berg Collection, The New York Public Library), Heather Moore (Harry Ransom Humanities Research Center, The University of Texas at Austin), R.N.R. Peers (Dorset County Museum), Charles E. Pierce Jr. and Inge Dupont (Pierpont Morgan Library), Michael Plunkett and Adrienne Cannon (University of Virginia Library), and Gene K. Rinkel (University Library, University of Illinois at Urbana-Champaign). Also Beth Crockett (A.P. Watt Ltd.), Julie Fallowfield (McIntosh and Otis, Inc.), William Heinemann Ltd., Harold Ober Associates,

Inc., Gerald J. Pollinger (Laurence Pollinger Ltd.), The Society of Authors, and Richard L. Underwood (Walker Martineau Ltd.).

I thank Richard Kent, Julian Bach, Cynthia Barrett, Norman Stahl and Yester Ensign for their wise counsel.

GREAT BEGINNINGS

1 ❦ INTRODUCTION

"I don't know if you have had the same experience, but the snag I always come up against when I'm telling a story is this dashed difficult problem of where to begin it," confides P. G. Wodehouse's winsome dilettante, Bertie Wooster, on the first page of one of the classic Jeeves novels, *Right Ho, Jeeves.* "It's a thing you don't want to go wrong over, because one false step and you're sunk. I mean, if you fool about too long at the start, trying to establish atmosphere, as they call it, and all that sort of rot, you fail to grip and the customers walk out on you."

If Wodehouse shared this problem with his guileless character, which is probable, but still difficult to believe, he knew how to find the solution. *Right Ho, Jeeves* begins with a deceptively simple first line directed to the inimitable gentleman's gentleman that promises Wodehouse cognoscenti hours of sophisticated silliness:

"'Jeeves,' I said, 'may I speak frankly?'"

Every novelist, from the absolute novice to Thomas Hardy, Ernest Hemingway, and Norman Mailer, has known the exciting but intimidating challenge of that first sentence, the imperative to grip a reader's attention sufficiently to carry him on through the only slightly less daunting second sentence into the next paragraph and to the end of the page. Everyone has had to begin somewhere.

Vita Sackville-West began *her* novel, *The Edwardians,* by writing about—how to begin a novel. "Among the many problems which beset the novelist, not the least weighty is the choice of the moment at which to begin his novel," the book opens. "It is necessary, it is indeed unavoidable, that he should intersect the lives of his dramatis personae at a given hour; all that remains is to decide which hour it shall be, and in what situation they shall be discovered." There were not only the life and the death of the character to consider as starting points, but a whole continuum of episodes and circumstances, hours and moments, from which to choose. Any of them might be valid, but the novelist could select only one.

So, where to begin?

Some novelists have strolled unhurriedly into their stories, some leaped directly into the action, some have found a few words sufficient, some an entire page. Some first lines are so remarkable they have become memorable as famous quotations. Surely Herman Melville as he wrote, "Call me Ishmael," or Charles Dickens, as he dipped his pen and began, "It was the best of times, it was the worst of times ...," must have smiled with satisfaction. There is little doubt when it is right.

And when it is wrong. For the lack of just the right first line, novels have languished unwritten. And although it is obvious that an opening that proved exactly right for Joseph Conrad or for William Faulkner would not have been possible for Anthony Burgess or John Updike (and even inconceivable that *Lord Jim* could have begun as *Nostromo* does), yet it is illuminating to compare the techniques novelists have used and the choices they have made.

Great Beginnings is intended to bring the delight of recognition to all readers of novels—whether writers or not—by recalling some of the great beginning sentences of novels that have achieved distinction and reputation. However, if you are a promising novelist wondering how to begin, reading through this collection of opening lines may give you the courage and the inspiration you need, by showing you the simplicity and variety of some of the solutions to the writer's dilemma that others have found. Each excerpt includes just enough to indicate where the beginning is leading, and to show how the author contrived to follow that first, miraculous thought. For the sake of easy comparison, selections have been grouped into categories that illustrate how authors widely separated by style, culture, and time—even centuries—have relied upon surprisingly similar techniques.

If the excerpts are unsatisfying in any way, it is because they are incomplete; they are not meant to stand alone. In fact, it is an indication of their success that we want to read more of some books we may never have considered taking off a shelf. In this way, *Great Beginnings* quite naturally forms a solid and varied reading list, encompassing authors from the beginning of the nineteenth century—when the novel as we have come to know it took form under the pens of Jane Austen and Sir Walter Scott—to the present. Although concentrating on English-speaking authors, the book includes the work of novelists writing in other languages when omission would leave serious gaps. How could one ignore, for instance, *Madame Bovary, War and Peace,* or *Buddenbrooks*?

Of course, *Great Beginnings* makes no claim to be exhaustive, and although an effort has been made to include the great classics of literature, inevitably personal favorites may be missing. It is, however, a great beginning.

2 ❧ ONCE UPON A TIME

he novel is, first of all, the telling of a story. Whether it begins at the beginning with the birth of a hero, at the end with his death, or somewhere in the middle in his youth or his prime as he approaches the event that will differentiate his life from all others, a story must be told. Who is to tell it— the hero or heroine, a casual witness, the author–creator himself, or the author masquerading as another writer—is one of the first choices the novelist must make.

In most cases, the choice is an unconscious one. For although it is perhaps simplistic to say that the story dictates its own teller, the novel probably *does* "come" to the author in one of these voices, just as a story suggests itself to a writer as a novel, rather than a play or a film. And so, *Great Expectations* and *The Magus* are narrated by their heroes, *Moby-Dick* and *My Ántonia* are related by witnesses, and *The Portrait of a*

Lady and *Tess of the d'Urbervilles* are told by their authors.

Of course, each of these novels could have been told from another point of view. Witness the recent successful retelling of Stevenson's *Dr. Jekyll and Mr. Hyde* through the eyes of the housemaid instead of the lawyer, Mr. Utterson. Or the attempted re-creation, by means of a letter from Heathcliff, of the years Heathcliff was mysteriously absent from Wuthering Heights, in the novel *H*. But although other approaches were possible, they would have resulted in very different stories. *Wuthering Heights* might have been much more interesting psychologically if Emily Brontë had chosen to allow Heathcliff to tell his own story. But she knew instinctively that the strange blackness of his personality was far more effectively revealed from the innocent lips of the housekeeper, Nelly Dean, and the tenant, Mr. Lockwood. On the other hand, *Rebecca* told in the words of the second Mrs. de Winter forces us to experience her growing fears in a way that would not be as possible with the intervention of a narrator. Conversely, the vast Russian tapestry of *War and Peace* could never have been woven in such brilliant detail by a girlish Natasha (or even by a Pierre, despite his infatuation with Napoleon); it required the omniscience of the novelist. In each of these novels, the chosen point of view is well-suited to the requirements of the story.

Storytelling through the ages has depended upon these three points of view. Which is the most natural? Is it the story told in the first person by the actor of the drama, with the intimacy of a confession? "As soon as I got to Borstal they made me a long-distance cross-country runner. I suppose they thought I was just the build for it because I was long and skinny for my age (and still am) and in any case I didn't mind it much, to tell you the truth, because running had always been made much of in our family, especially running away from the police" (Alan Sillitoe, *The Loneliness of the Long-distance Runner*). Is it the story confided by the witness, who shapes the character and the plot by what he chooses to tell and not tell? "I had the story, bit by bit, from various people, and, as generally happens in such cases, each time it was a different story" (Edith Wharton, *Ethan Frome*). Or is it the story told from the omniscient point-of-view of the author, in the tradition of once-upon-a-time? "There once lived, in a sequestered part of the county of Devonshire, one Mr. Godfrey Nickleby, a worthy gentleman, who, taking it into his head rather late in life that he must get married, and not being young enough or rich enough to aspire to the hand of a lady of fortune, had wedded an old flame out of mere attachment, who in her turn had taken him for the same reason" (Charles Dickens, *Life and Adventures of Nicholas Nickleby*). Each is a totally valid choice, but although it may sound somewhat mysterious, in the end it is usually the story that determines the storyteller.

The selections in this chapter show how novelists have used two of these voices: narration by the main character, and narration by a witness. The third, narration by the author, which presents many more options to the writer, is illustrated by most of the chapters that follow.

The First Person in Person ∿
The hero tells the story in his own words.

I was born in 1927, the only child of middle-class parents, both English, and themselves born in the grotesquely elongated shadow, which they never rose sufficiently above history to leave, of that monstrous dwarf Queen Victoria. I was sent to a public school, I wasted two years doing my national service, I went to Oxford; and there I began to discover I was not the person I wanted to be.

—JOHN FOWLES, *The Magus*

I was born poor in rich America, yet my secret instincts were better than money and were for me a source of power. I had advantages that no one could take away from me—a clear memory and brilliant dreams and a knack for knowing when I was happy.

—PAUL THEROUX, *My Secret History*

I wasn't born yet so it was Cousin Gowan who was there and big enough to see and remember and tell me afterward when I was big enough for it to make sense. That is, it was Cousin Gowan plus Uncle Gavin or maybe Uncle Gavin rather plus Cousin Gowan. He—Cousin Gowan—was thirteen.

—WILLIAM FAULKNER, *The Town*

Whether I shall turn out to be the hero of my own life, or whether that station will be held by anybody else, these pages must show. To begin my life with the beginning of my life, I record that I was born (as I have been informed and believe) on a Friday, at twelve o'clock at night. It was remarked that the clock began to strike, and I began to cry, simultaneously.

—CHARLES DICKENS,
The Personal History of David Copperfield

If you really want to hear about it, the first thing you'll probably want to know is where I was born, and what my lousy childhood was like, and how my parents were occupied and all before they had me, and all that David Copperfield kind of crap, but I don't feel like going into it, if you want to know the truth.

—J. D. SALINGER, *The Catcher in the Rye*

I am an American, Chicago born—Chicago, that somber city—and go at things as I have taught myself, free-style, and will make the record in my own way: first to knock, first admitted; sometimes an innocent knock, sometimes a not so innocent. But a man's character is his fate, says Heraclitus, and in the end there isn't any way to disguise the nature of the knocks by acoustical work on the door or gloving the knuckles.

—SAUL BELLOW, *The Adventures of Augie March*

Though I haven't ever been on the screen I was brought up in pictures. Rudolph Valentino came to my fifth birthday party—or so I was told. I put this down only to indicate that even before the age of reason I was in a position to watch the wheels go round.

—F. SCOTT FITZGERALD, *The Last Tycoon*

My wound is geography. It is also my anchorage, my port of call.

I grew up slowly beside the tides and marshes of Colleton; my arms were tawny and strong from working long days on the shrimp boat in the blazing South Carolina heat. Because I was a Wingo, I worked as soon as I could walk; I could pick a blue crab clean when I was five. I had killed my first deer by the age of seven, and at nine was regularly putting meat on my family's table. I was born and raised on a Carolina sea island and I carried the sunshine of the low-country, inked in dark gold, on my back and shoulders.

—PAT CONROY, Prologue, *The Prince of Tides*

My first vision of earth was water veiled. I am of the race of men and women who see all things through this curtain of sea, and my eyes are the color of water.

I looked with chameleon eyes upon the changing face of the world, looked with anonymous vision upon my uncompleted self.

I remember my first birth in water. All round me a sulphurous transparency and my bones move as if made of rubber. I sway and float, stand on boneless toes listening for distant sounds, sounds beyond the reach of human ears, see things beyond the reach of human eyes.

—ANAÏS NIN, *House of Incest*

Call me Jonah. My parents did, or nearly did. They called me John.

Jonah—John—if I had been a Sam, I would have been a Jonah still—not because I have been unlucky for others, but because somebody or something has compelled me to be certain places at certain times, without fail. Conveyances and motives, both conventional and bizarre, have been provided. And, according to plan, at each appointed second, at each appointed place this Jonah was there.

—KURT VONNEGUT, JR., *Cat's Cradle*

George is my name; my deeds have been heard of in Tower Hall, and my childhood has been chronicled in the *Journal of Experimental Psychology.* I am he that was called in those days Billy Bocksfuss—cruel misnomer. For had I indeed a cloven foot I'd not now hobble upon a stick or need ride pick-a-back to class in humid weather.

—JOHN BARTH, *Giles Goat-Boy*

My name is George Smith. I get up on the right side of the bed every morning because I pushed the left to the wall. I'm in business. I sleep naked between the sheets. And these days always alone unless for accidental encounters.

—J. P. DONLEAVY, *A Singular Man*

My father's family name being Pirrip, and my Christian name Philip, my infant tongue could make of both names nothing longer or more explicit than Pip. So I called myself Pip, and came to be called Pip.

I give Pirrip as my father's family name on the authority of his tombstone and my sister—Mrs. Joe Gargery, who married the blacksmith.

—CHARLES DICKENS, *Great Expectations*

You don't know about me, without you have read a book by the name of "The Adventures of Tom Sawyer," but that ain't no matter. That book was made by Mr. Mark Twain, and he told the truth, mainly. There was things which he stretched, but mainly he told the truth. That is nothing. I never seen anybody but lied, one time or another, without it was Aunt Polly, or the widow, or maybe Mary. Aunt Polly—Tom's Aunt Polly, she is—and Mary, and the Widow Douglas, is all told about in that book—which is mostly a true book; with some stretchers, as I said before.

—MARK TWAIN, *Adventures of Huckleberry Finn*

The first page of the original manuscript of Charles Dickens's
Great Expectations. (Wisbech and Fenland Museum)

Granted: I am an inmate of a mental hospital; my keeper is watching me, he never lets me out of his sight; there's a peephole in the door, and my keeper's eye is the shade of brown that can never see through a blue-eyed type like me.

So you see, my keeper can't be an enemy. I've come to be very fond of him; when he stops looking at me from behind the door and comes into the room, I tell him incidents from my life, so he can get to know me in spite of the peephole between us.

—GÜNTER GRASS, *The Tin Drum,* trans. Ralph Manheim

I will begin the story of my adventures with a certain morning early in the month of June, the year of grace 1751, when I took the key for the last time out of the door of my father's house. The sun began to shine upon the summit of the hills as I went down the road; and by the time I had come as far as the manse, the blackbirds were whistling in the garden lilacs, and the mist that hung around the valley in the time of the dawn was beginning to arise and die away.

—ROBERT LOUIS STEVENSON, *Kidnapped*

I am going to pack my two shirts with my other socks and my best suit in the little blue cloth my mother used to tie round her hair when she did the house, and I am going from the Valley.

This cloth is much too good to pack things in and I would keep it in my pocket only there is nothing else in the house

that will serve, and the lace straw basket is over at Mr. Tom
Harries', over the mountain. If I went down to Tossall the
Shop for a cardboard box I would have to tell him why I
wanted it, then everybody would know I was going.

—RICHARD LLEWELLYN, *How Green Was My Valley*

As soon as I got to Borstal they made me a long-distance
cross-country runner. I suppose they thought I was just the
build for it because I was long and skinny for my age (and
still am) and in any case I didn't mind it much, to tell you
the truth, because running had always been made much of in
our family, especially running away from the police.

—ALAN SILLITOE, *The Loneliness of the Long-distance Runner*

For a long time I used to go to bed early. Sometimes, when I
had put out my candle, my eyes would close so quickly that I
had not even time to say "I'm going to sleep." And half an
hour later the thought that it was time to go to sleep would
awaken me; I would try to put away the book which, I
imagined, was still in my hands, and to blow out the light; I
had been thinking all the time, while I was asleep, of what I
had just been reading, but my thoughts had run into a channel of their own, until I myself seemed actually to have
become the subject of my book: a church, a quartet, the
rivalry between François I and Charles V. This impression
would persist for some moments after I was awake; it did not
disturb my mind, but it lay like scales upon my eyes and pre-

vented them from registering the fact that the candle was no
longer burning.

> —MARCEL PROUST,
> *Swann's Way,* trans. C. K. Scott Moncrieff

A strange melancholy pervades me to which I hesitate to
give the grave and beautiful name of sorrow. The idea of sorrow has always appealed to me, but now I am almost
ashamed of its complete egoism. I have known boredom,
regret, and occasionally remorse, but never sorrow. Today it
envelops me like a silken web, enervating and soft, and sets
me apart from everybody else.

> —FRANÇOISE SAGAN, *Bonjour Tristesse,* trans. Irene Ash

I stand at the window of this great house in the south of
France as night falls, the night which is leading me to the
most terrible morning of my life. I have a drink in my hand,
there is a bottle at my elbow. I watch my reflection in the
darkening gleam of the window pane. My reflection is tall,
perhaps rather like an arrow, my blond hair gleams. My face
is like a face you have seen many times.

> —JAMES BALDWIN, *Giovanni's Room*

I came to Warley on a wet September morning with the sky
the grey of Guiseley sandstone. I was alone in the compart-

ment. I remember saying to myself: "No more zombies, Joe, no more zombies."

—JOHN BRAINE, *Room at the Top*

It came down to this: if I had not been arrested by the Turkish police, I would have been arrested by the Greek police. I had no choice but to do as this man Harper told me. He was entirely responsible for what happened to me.

—ERIC AMBLER, *The Light of Day*

In my younger and more vulnerable years my father gave me some advice that I've been turning over in my mind ever since.

"Whenever you feel like criticizing any one," he told me, "just remember that all the people in this world haven't had the advantages that you've had."

He didn't say any more, but we've always been unusually communicative in a reserved way, and I understood that he meant a great deal more than that. In consequence, I'm inclined to reserve all judgments, a habit that has opened up many curious natures to me and also made me the victim of not a few veteran bores.

—F. SCOTT FITZGERALD, *The Great Gatsby*

Some advice

gave

Whenever

told me

haven't

all the people

IN my younger and more vulnerable years my father told me something that I've been turning over in my mind ever since.

"Whed you feel like criticising any one," he said, "just remember that everybody in this world hasn't had the advantages that you've had."

He didn't say any more, but we've always been unusually communicative in a reserved way, and I understood that he meant a great deal more than that. In consequence, I'm inclined to reserve all judgments, a habit that has opened up many curious natures to me and also made me the victim of not a few veteran bores. The abnormal mind is quick to detect and attach itself to this quality when it appears in a normal person, and so it came about that in college I was unjustly accused of being a politician, because I was privy to the secret griefs of wild, unknown men. Most of the confidences were unsought—frequently I have feigned sleep, preoccupation, or a hostile levity when I realized by some unmistakable sign that an intimate revelation was quivering on the horizon; for the intimate revelations of young men, or at least the terms in which they express them, are usually plagiaristic and marred by obvious suppressions. Reserving judgments is a matter of infinite hope. I am still a little afraid of missing something if I forget that, as my father snobbishly suggested, and I snobbishly repeat, a sense of the fundamental decencies is parcelled out unequally at birth.

And, after boasting this way of my tolerance, I come to the admission that it has a limit. Conduct may be founded on the hard rock or the wet marshes, but after a certain point I don't care what it's founded on. When I came back from the East last autumn I felt that I wanted the world to be in uniform and at a sort of moral attention forever; I wanted no more riotous excursions with privileged glimpses into the human heart. *Only* It was only Gatsby, the man who gives his name to this book, that was exempted from my reaction—Gatsby, who represented everything for which I have an unaffected scorn. If personality is an unbroken series of successful gestures, then there was something gorgeous about him, some heightened sensitivity to the promises of life, as if he were related to one of those intricate machines that register earthquakes ten thousand miles away. This responsiveness had nothing to do with that flabby impressionability which is dignified under the name of the "creative temperament"—it was an extraordinary gift for hope, a romantic readiness such as I have never found in any other person and which it is not likely I shall ever find again. No—Gatsby turned out all right at the end; it is what preyed on Gatsby, what foul dust floated in the wake of his dreams that temporarily closed out my interest in the abortive sorrows and unjustified elations of men.

except

First galley page of F. Scott Fitzgerald's *The Great Gatsby*, with further revisions in hand by the author. *(Princeton University Libraries)*

The Witness as Storyteller ⁓
The story through the eyes of a character who acts as narrator.

Call me Ishmael. Some years ago—never mind how long precisely—having little or no money in my purse, and nothing particular to interest me on shore, I thought I would sail about a little and see the watery part of the world. It is a way I have of driving off the spleen, and regulating the circulation. Whenever I find myself growing grim about the mouth; whenever it is a damp, drizzly November in my soul; whenever I find myself involuntarily pausing before coffin warehouses, and bringing up the rear of every funeral I meet; and especially whenever my hypos get such an upper hand of me, that it requires a strong moral principle to prevent me from deliberately stepping into the street, and methodically knocking people's hats off—then, I account it high time to get to sea as soon as I can.

—HERMAN MELVILLE, *Moby-Dick; or, The Whale*

I had the story, bit by bit, from various people, and, as generally happens in such cases, each time it was a different story.

If you know Starkfield, Massachusetts, you know the post-office. If you know the post-office you must have seen Ethan Frome drive up to it, drop the reins on his hollow-backed bay and drag himself across the brick pavement to the white colonnade: and you must have asked who he was.

—EDITH WHARTON, *Ethan Frome*

I first heard of Ántonia on what seemed to me an interminable journey across the great midland plain of North America. I was ten years old then; I had lost both my father and mother within a year, and my Virginia relatives were sending me out to my grandparents, who lived in Nebraska. I travelled in the care of a mountain boy, Jake Marpole, one of the "hands" on my father's old farm under the Blue Ridge, who was now going West to work for my grandfather. Jake's experience of the world was not much wider than mine. He had never been in a railway train until the morning when we set out together to try our fortunes in a new world.

—WILLA CATHER, *My Ántonia*

I will be her witness.

That would translate *seré su testigo,* and will not appear in your travelers' phrasebook because it is not a useful phrase for the prudent traveler.

Here is what happened: she left one man, she left a second man, she traveled again with the first; she let him die alone. She lost one child to "history" and another to "complications" (I offer in each instance the evaluation of others), she imagined herself capable of shedding that baggage and came to Boca Grande, a tourist. *Una turista.* So she said. In fact she came here less a tourist than a sojourner but she did not make that distinction.

—JOAN DIDION, *A Book of Common Prayer*

It was at a love-spinning that I saw Kester first. And if, in these new-fangled days, when strange inventions crowd upon us, when I hear tell there is even a machine coming into use in some parts of the country for reaping and mowing, if those that mayhappen will read this don't know what a love-spinning was, they shall hear in good time. But though it was Jancis Beguildy's love-spinning, she being three-and-twenty at that time and I being two years less, yet that is not the beginning of the story I have set out to tell.

—MARY WEBB, *Precious Bane*

I confess that when first I made acquaintance with Charles Strickland I never for a moment discerned that there was in him anything out of the ordinary. Yet now few will be found to deny his greatness. I do not speak of that greatness which is achieved by the fortunate politician or the successful soldier; that is a quality which belongs to the place he occupies rather than to the man; and a change of circumstances reduces it to very discreet proportions. The Prime Minister out of office is seen, too often, to have been but a pompous rhetorician, and the General without an army is but the tame hero of a market town. The greatness of Charles Strickland was authentic.

—W. SOMERSET MAUGHAM, *The Moon and Sixpence*

Later he was to be famous and honoured throughout the South Caribbean; he was to be a hero of the people and after that, a British representative at Lake Success. But when I first met him he was still a struggling masseur, at a time when masseurs were ten a penny in Trinidad.

—V. S. NAIPAUL, *The Mystic Masseur*

For the first fifteen years of our lives, Danny and I lived within five blocks of each other and neither of us knew of the other's existence.

Danny's block was heavily populated by the followers of his father, Russian Hasidic Jews in somber garb, whose habits and frames of reference were born on the soil of the land they had abandoned.

—CHAIM POTOK, *The Chosen*

This is the saddest story I have ever heard. We had known the Ashburnhams for nine seasons of the town of Nauheim with an extreme intimacy—or, rather, with an acquaintanceship as loose and easy and yet as close as a good glove's with your hand. My wife and I knew Captain and Mrs. Ashburnham as well as it was possible to know anybody, and yet, in another sense, we knew nothing at all about them. This is, I believe, a state of things only possible with English people of whom, till today, when I sit down to puzzle out what I know of this sad affair, I knew nothing whatever.

—FORD MADOX FORD, *The Good Soldier*

1801.—I have just returned from a visit to my landlord—the solitary neighbour that I shall be troubled with. This is certainly, a beautiful country! In all England, I do not believe that I could have fixed on a situation so completely removed from the stir of society. A perfect misanthropist's Heaven—and Mr Heathcliff and I are such a suitable pair to divide the desolation between us. A capital fellow! He little imagined how my heart warmed towards him when I beheld his black eyes withdraw so suspiciously under their brows, as I rode up, and when his fingers sheltered themselves, with a jealous resolution, still further in his waistcoat, as I announced my name.

'Mr Heathcliff?' I said.

A nod was the answer.

—EMILY BRONTË, *Wuthering Heights*

We were in class when the headmaster came in, followed by a new boy, not wearing the school uniform, and a school servant carrying a large desk. Those who had been asleep woke up, and every one rose as if just surprised at his work.

The headmaster made a sign to us to sit down. Then, turning to the teacher, he said to him in a low voice:

"Monsieur Roger, here is a pupil whom I recommend to your care; he'll be in the second. If his work and conduct are satisfactory, he will go into one of the upper classes, as becomes his age."

—GUSTAVE FLAUBERT, *Madame Bovary,* trans. Paul de Man, based on version by Eleanor Marx Aveling

In undertaking to describe the recent and strange incidents in our town, till lately wrapped in uneventful obscurity, I find myself forced in absence of literary skill to begin my story rather far back, that is to say, with certain biographical details concerning that talented and highly-esteemed gentleman, Stepan Trofimovich Verhovensky.

—FYODOR DOSTOYEVSKY,
The Possessed, trans. Constance Garnett

If anybody cares to read a simple tale told simply, I, John Ridd, of the parish of Oare, in the county of Somerset, yeoman and churchwarden, have seen and had a share in some doings of this neighborhood, which I will try to set down in order, God sparing my life and memory. And they who light upon this book should bear in mind, not only that I write for the clearing of our parish from ill-fame and calumny, but also a thing which will, I trow, appear too often in it, to wit—that I am nothing more than a plain unlettered man, not read in foreign languages, as a gentleman might be, nor gifted with long words (even in mine own tongue), save what I may have won from the Bible, or Master William Shakespeare, whom in the face of common opinion, I do value highly. In short, I am an ignoramus, but pretty well for a yeoman.

—R. D. BLACKMORE, *Lorna Doone*

When I think of all the grey memorials erected in London to equestrian generals, the heroes of old colonial wars, and to frock-coated politicians who are even more deeply forgotten, I can find no reason to mock the modest stone that commemorates Jones on the far side of the international road which he failed to cross in a country far from home, though I am not to this day absolutely sure of where, geographically speaking, Jones's home lay. At least he paid for the monument—however unwillingly—with his life, while the generals as a rule came home safe and paid, if at all, with the blood of their men, and as for the politicians—who cares for dead politicians sufficiently to remember with what issues they were identified? Free Trade is less interesting than an Ashanti war, though the London pigeons do not distinguish between the two. *Exegi monumentum.* Whenever my rather bizarre business takes me north to Monte Cristi and I pass the stone, I feel a certain pride that my action helped to raise it.

—GRAHAM GREENE, *The Comedians*

I had even reached the point of wondering if Geraldine Brevoort's suicide, so long dreaded, might not prove in the event a relief, but like everything else about Geraldine, when it came, it came with a nasty twist. She had plagued me living; now, apparently, she would plague me dead.

—LOUIS AUCHINCLOSS, *Portrait in Brownstone*

In the days when I lived in Hecate County, I had an uncomfortable neighbor, a man named Asa M. Stryker. He had at one time, he told me, taught chemistry in some sooty-sounding college in Pennsylvania, but he now lived on a little money which he had been "lucky enough to inherit." I had the feeling about him that somewhere in the background was defeat or frustration or disgrace.

—EDMUND WILSON, *Memoirs of Hecate County*

Kit didn't speak much or often of her father. "Pap," she sometimes called him and sometimes she spoke of him as "Father." After all, Kit when I knew her had been made over in the big world. She had her knowing, her way of knowing, and it seemed to me more real than most of the ways of knowing most of us have.

And then, too, she was wanting something not culture, in the restricted sense. "The hell with that," would have been her word.

Her story came to me in fragments. We were together for that purpose, that I might get her story as one more of the multitude of curious, terrible, silly, absorbing or wonderful stories all people could tell if they knew how.

—SHERWOOD ANDERSON, *Kit Brandon*

3 The Author Intrudes

It was common for nineteenth century novelists to address their readers directly—usually as "dear reader"—to tell them what to expect from the story that was to follow, or what their own feelings or limitations were in writing it. Such an intrusion placed them above and apart from their characters, a relationship that brings to mind the Hirshfeld cartoon for the stage production of *My Fair Lady,* which depicted Bernard Shaw manipulating Henry Higgins and Eliza Doolittle on marionette strings. In the drawing, Shaw looks suspiciously like God, and in a sense, the author acts as God when he intrudes on the story he is telling: he reminds us that *he* or *she* is the Creator of the characters we are about to meet.

Although this approach is not used as often today, it still has the same effect: it gives the "dear reader" the feeling that the author has placed an arm around his shoulder, and is about to confide something to him alone. "With a single drop of ink for a mirror, the Egyptian sorcerer undertakes to reveal to any chance comer far-reaching visions of the past. This is what I undertake to do for you, reader," begins George Eliot's *Adam Bede*. Once the reader is in the author's confidence and the story or the hero has been introduced, the intimacy of the first person is abandoned, and the story begins to move on its own.

Sometimes the author masks himself by assuming the identity of another, fictional "writer," as Robert Louis Stevenson did in *Treasure Island*: "Squire Trelawney, Dr. Livesey, and the rest of these gentlemen having asked me to write down the whole particulars about Treasure Island, from the beginning to the end, keeping nothing back but the bearings of the island, and that only because there is still treasure not yet lifted, I take up my pen in the year of grace 17—..." Or the author pretends to be the discoverer of a manuscript written by someone else. "The writer of this singular autobiography was my cousin, who died at the———Criminal Lunatic Asylum, of which he had been an inmate three years," begins George du Maurier's *Peter Ibbetson*. The faux-author is simply an "editor," and usually takes pains to disclaim responsibility for the contents, as well as for the quality, of the writing. Thus we can enjoy the irony of Conrad, the consummate stylist, writing, in *Under Western Eyes*: "To begin with I wish to disclaim the possession of those high gifts of imagination and expression which would have enabled my pen to create for the reader the personality of the man who called himself, after the Russian custom, Cyril son of Isidor—Kirylo Sidorovitch—Razumov."

Frequently, the author's statement of his intentions for the novel, or the faux-author's introduction of the manuscript, journal, or letters on which the novel is based, is kept to a preface (or "prologue" or "introduction" as it is called in *Peter Ibbetson*). As distinguished from the prefatory note written and signed by the author, this preface is a part of the novel, and adds valuable information to the story. It is the author playing hide and seek with his reader.

The Author and Faux-Author ∽
The author introduces his story—as himself and in disguise as another.

I have never begun a novel with more misgiving. If I call it a novel it is only because I don't know what else to call it. I have little story to tell and I end neither with a death nor a marriage. Death ends all things and so is the comprehensive conclusion of a story, but marriage finishes it very properly too and the sophisticated are ill-advised to sneer at what is by convention termed a happy ending. It is a sound instinct of the common people which persuades them that with this all that needs to be said is said. When male and female, after whatever vicissitudes you like, are at last brought together they have fulfilled their biological function and interest passes to the generation that is to come. But I leave my reader in the air. This book consists of my recollections of a man with whom I was thrown into close contact only at long intervals, and I have little knowledge of what happened to him in between. I suppose that by the exercise of invention I could fill the gaps plausibly enough and so make my narrative more coherent; but I have no wish to do that. I only want to set down what I know of my own knowledge.

—W. SOMERSET MAUGHAM, *The Razor's Edge*

Reader, I am going to tell you the story of Clifford, Helen and little Nell. Helen and Clifford wanted everything for Nell and wanted it so much and so badly their daughter was in great danger of ending up with nothing at all, not even life. If you want a great deal for yourself it is only natural to want the same for your children. Alas, the two are not necessarily compatible.

—FAY WELDON, *The Hearts and Lives of Men*

Let the reader be introduced to Lady Carbury, upon whose character and doings much will depend of whatever interest these pages may have, as she sits at her writing-table in her own room in her own house in Welbeck Street. Lady Carbury spent many hours at her desk, and wrote many letters,—wrote also very much besides letters. She spoke of

herself in these days as a woman devoted to Literature, always
spelling the word with a big L.
　　　　　　　—ANTHONY TROLLOPE, *The Way We Live Now*

The opening chapter does not concern itself with Love—
indeed that antagonist does not certainly appear until the
third—and Mr. Lewisham is seen at his studies. It was ten
years ago, and in those days he was assistant master in the
Whortley Proprietary School, Whortley, Sussex, and his
wages were forty pounds a year, out of which he had to
afford fifteen shillings a week during term time to lodge with
Mrs. Munday, at the little shop in the West Street.
　　　　　　　—H. G. WELLS, *Love and Mr. Lewisham*

Our story opens in the mind of Luther L. (L for LeRoy)
Fliegler, who is lying in his bed, not thinking of anything,
but just aware of sounds, conscious of his own breathing, and
sensitive to his own heartbeats. Lying beside him is his wife,
lying on her right side and enjoying her sleep
　　　　　　　—JOHN O'HARA, *Appointment in Samarra*

With a single drop of ink for a mirror, the Egyptian sorcerer
undertakes to reveal to any chance comer far-reaching
visions of the past. This is what I undertake to do for you,
reader. With this drop of ink at the end of my pen, I will
show you the roomy workshop of Mr. Jonathan Burge, car-

penter and builder, in the village of Hayslope, as it appeared
on the eighteenth of June, in the year of our Lord 1799.

—GEORGE ELIOT, *Adam Bede*

It has occurred to the writer to call this unimportant history
The Green Hat because a green hat was the first thing about
her that he saw: as also it was, in a way, the last thing about
her that he saw. It was bright green, of a sort of felt, and
bravely worn: being, no doubt, one of those that women
who have many hats affect *pour le sport*.

—MICHAEL ARLEN, *The Green Hat*

This is a true story but I can't believe it's really happening.
    It's a murder story, too. I can't believe my luck.
    And a love story (I think), of all strange things, so late in
the century, so late in the goddamned day.

—MARTIN AMIS, *London Fields*

There are certain things that I feel, as I look through this
bundle of manuscript, that I must say. The first is that of
course no writer ever has fulfilled his intention and no writer
ever will; secondly, that there was, when I began, another
intention than that of dealing with my subject adequately,
namely that of keeping myself outside the whole of it; I was
to be, in the most abstract and immaterial sense of the word,
a voice, and that simply because this business of seeing Rus-

sian psychology through English eyes has no excuse except
that it *is* English.

—HUGH WALPOLE, *The Secret City*

In any memoir it is usual for the first sentence to reveal as
much as possible of your subject's nature by illustrating it in a
vivid and memorable motto, and with my own first sentence
now drawing to a finish I see I have failed to do this! But
writing is made with the fingers, and all writing, even the
clumsy kind, exposes in its loops and slants a yearning deeper
than an intention, the soul of the writer flapping on the
clothespin of his exclamation mark. Including the sentence
scribbled above: being slow to disclose my nature is characteristic of me. So I am not off to such a bad start after all.
My mutters make me remember. Later, I will talk about my
girls.

—PAUL THEROUX, *Saint Jack*

To begin with I wish to disclaim the possession of those high
gifts of imagination and expression which would have
enabled my pen to create for the reader the personality of the
man who called himself, after the Russian custom, Cyril son
of Isidor—Kirylo Sidorovitch—Razumov.

If I have ever had these gifts in any sort of living form they
have been smothered out of existence a long time ago under
a wilderness of words. Words, as is well known, are the great
foes of reality. I have been for many years a teacher of lan-

guages. It is an occupation which at length becomes fatal to whatever share of imagination, observation, and insight an ordinary person may be heir to. To a teacher of languages there comes a time when the world is but a place of many words and man appears a mere talking animal not much more wonderful than a parrot.

—JOSEPH CONRAD, *Under Western Eyes*

The writer of this singular autobiography was my cousin, who died at the————Criminal Lunatic Asylum, of which he had been an inmate three years.

—GEORGE DU MAURIER, Introduction, *Peter Ibbetson*

I am but a poor scribe, ill-versed in the craft of wielding words and phrases, as the cultivated reader (if I should ever happen to have one) will no doubt very soon find out for himself.

—Part One, *Peter Ibbetson*

Squire Trelawney, Dr. Livesey, and the rest of these gentlemen having asked me to write down the whole particulars about Treasure Island, from the beginning to the end, keeping nothing back but the bearings of the island, and that only because there is still treasure not yet lifted, I take up my pen in the year of grace 17—and go back to the time when my father kept the Admiral Benbow inn and the brown old sea-man with the sabre cut first took up his lodging under our roof.

I remember him as if it were yesterday, as he came plodding to the inn door, his sea-chest following behind him in a hand-barrow—a tall, strong, heavy, nut-brown man, his tarry pigtail falling over the shoulders of his soiled blue coat, his hands ragged and scarred, with black, broken nails, and the sabre cut across one cheek, a dirty, livid white.

—ROBERT LOUIS STEVENSON, *Treasure Island*

The first ray of light which illumines the gloom, and con-verts into a dazzling brilliancy that obscurity in which the earlier history of the public career of the immortal Pickwick would appear to be involved, is derived from the perusal of the following entry in the Transactions of the Pickwick Club, which the editor of these papers feels the highest plea-sure in laying before his readers as a proof of the careful attention, indefatigable assiduity, and nice discrimination with which his search among the multi-farious documents confided to him has been conducted.

"May 12, 1827. Joseph Smiggers, Esq.,P.V.P.M.P.C.,* presiding. The following resolutions unanimously agreed to:"
*Perpetual Vice-President—Member Pickwick Club.

—CHARLES DICKENS, *The Pickwick Papers*

Editors' Note

These notebooks were found among the papers of Antoine Roquentin. They are published without alteration.

The first sheet is undated, but there is good reason to believe it was written some weeks before the diary itself. Thus it would have been written around the beginning of January, 1932, at the latest.

At that time, Antoine Roquentin, after travelling through Central Europe, North Africa and the Far East, settled in Bouville for three years to conclude his historical research on the Marquis de Rollebon.

The Editors
—Jean-Paul Sartre, *Nausea,*
trans. Lloyd Alexander

I had this story from one who had no business to tell it to me, or to any other. I may credit the seductive influence of an old vintage upon the narrator for the beginning of it, and my own skeptical incredulity during the days that followed for the balance of the strange tale.

When my convivial host discovered that he had told me so much, and that I was prone to doubtfulness, his foolish pride assumed the task the old vintage had commenced, and so he unearthed written evidence in the form of musty manuscript, and dry official records of the British Colonial Office, to support many of the salient features of his remarkable narrative.

—Edgar Rice Burroughs,
Tarzan of the Apes

George William Apley was born in the house of his maternal grandfather, William Leeds Hancock, on the steeper part of Mount Vernon Street, on Beacon Hill, on January 25, 1866. He died in his own house, which overlooks the Charles River Basin and the Esplanade, on the water side of Beacon Street, on December 13, 1933. This was the frame in which his life moved, and the frame which will surround his portrait as a man. He once said of himself: "I am the sort of man I am, because environment prevented my being anything else."

It is now my task, to which I have agreed under somewhat unusual circumstances, to depict the life of this valued friend of mine through his own writings.

—JOHN P. MARQUAND, *The Late George Apley*

4 ✣ ENTER THE HERO/HEROINE

lthough a novel can be suggested by a situation or a setting, it is more likely to come about because of a character the writer conceives as a hero or heroine. Whether the character bears a resemblance to the writer, in looks, traits, or beliefs, or conversely, is the kind of person the writer secretly admires (or despises), the hero/heroine exists because he or she has a personal significance to the author. For the novelist, identifying the bond that has drawn him to a particular hero or heroine is particularly important in clarifying the passion that will move the book. The bond may be a strongly-held belief, a common background, a sense of rebellion against life, a shared strength or weakness, but it must be relevant to the novelist for the character's essence to be communicated to the reader.

Often, the bond is love. For instance, the heroine of

Thomas Hardy's *A Pair of Blue Eyes* is drawn from his first wife, Emma Lavinia Gifford, and his *Tess of the d'Urbervilles* from a chance sighting of a Dorset milkmaid who captivated him. The impression was so strong that when, in his dotage, Hardy saw Tess come to life in a young actress portraying her in a local dramatization of the novel (the daughter of a woman who had worked at the same farm and, conceivably, "Tess's" daughter), he began an obsessive relationship with his own character, a relationship that his (second, much younger) wife jealously brought to an end.

The lifelikeness of a heroine like Hardy's Tess is one of the distinguishing characteristics of the modern novel. The romantic heroes and heroines of the eighteenth century bore as little resemblance to reality as did the world of melodrama and adventure they inhabited. As the novel progressed into the nineteenth century, however, these cardboard creations matured into living, believable characters who moved in realistic situations. Such characters may not be precisely true to life—a hero or heroine can be *more* noble or evil than a real-life counterpart might be expected to be—but they should act in a manner that is consistent and believable for that character.

Because the writer is so personally involved with the principal character, it is natural that many novels begin with a description of the hero or heroine. In fact, the first words of the novel are often the hero's name. "Scarlett O'Hara was not beautiful"; "Emma Woodhouse, handsome, clever, and rich"; "The Miss Lonelyhearts of the New York *Post-Dispatch*"; "Robert Cohn was once middleweight boxing champion of Princeton"; "Roy Hobbs pawed at the glass" all give the hero/heroine the first entrance. The same technique can also introduce a secondary character, or even a character whose only importance is establishing the setting for the book, and examples of these openings have also been included in this chapter.

Cynthia Turned, Her Eyes Smouldering ⁓
The immediate introduction of one or more of the book's main characters.

Scarlett O'Hara was not beautiful, but men seldom realized it when caught by her charm as the Tarleton twins were. In her face were too sharply blended the delicate features of her mother, a Coast aristocrat of French descent, and the heavy ones of her florid Irish father. But it was an arresting face, pointed of chin, square of jaw. Her eyes were pale green without a touch of hazel, starred with bristly black lashes and slightly tilted at the ends. Above them, her thick black brows slanted upward, cutting a startling oblique line in her magnolia-white skin—that skin so prized by Southern women and so carefully guarded with bonnets, veils and mittens against hot Georgia suns.
                        —MARGARET MITCHELL, *Gone With the Wind*

Robert Cohn was once middleweight boxing champion of Princeton. Do not think that I am very much impressed by that as a boxing title, but it meant a lot to Cohn. He cared nothing for boxing, in fact he disliked it, but he learned it painfully and thoroughly to counteract the feeling of inferiority and shyness he had felt on being treated as a Jew at Princeton. There was a certain inner comfort in knowing he could knock down anybody who was snooty to him, although, being very shy and a thoroughly nice boy, he never fought except in the gym.

—ERNEST HEMINGWAY, *The Sun Also Rises*

Emma Woodhouse, handsome, clever, and rich, with a comfortable home and happy disposition, seemed to unite some of the best blessings of existence, and had lived nearly twenty-one years in the world with very little to distress or vex her.

—JANE AUSTEN, *Emma*

The Miss Lonelyhearts of the New York *Post-Dispatch* (Are you in trouble?—Do-you-need-advice?—Write-to-Miss-Lonelyhearts-and-she-will-help-you) sat at his desk and stared at a piece of white cardboard. On it a prayer had been printed by Shrike, the feature editor.

—NATHANAEL WEST, *Miss Lonelyhearts*

Mr. Sherlock Holmes, who was usually very late in the mornings, save upon those not infrequent occasions when he was up all night, was seated at the breakfast table. I stood upon the hearth-rug and picked up the stick which our visitor had left behind him the night before. It was a fine, thick piece of wood, bulbous-headed, of the sort which is known as a "Penang lawyer."

—SIR ARTHUR CONAN DOYLE, *The Hound of the Baskervilles*

Elmer Gantry was drunk. He was eloquently drunk, lovingly and pugnaciously drunk. He leaned against the bar of the Old Home Sample Room, the most gilded and urbane saloon in Cato, Missouri, and requested the bartender to join him in "The Good Old Summer Time," the waltz of the day.

—SINCLAIR LEWIS, *Elmer Gantry*

Buck did not read the newspapers, or he would have known that trouble was brewing, not alone for himself, but for every tidewater dog, strong of muscle and with warm, long hair, from Puget Sound to San Diego. Because men, groping in the Arctic darkness, had found a yellow metal, and because steamship and transportation companies were booming the find, thousands of men were rushing into the Northland. These men wanted dogs, and the dogs they wanted were heavy dogs, with strong muscles by which to toil, and furry coats to protect them from the frost.

—JACK LONDON, *The Call of the Wild*

Mr. Phileas Fogg lived, in 1872, at No. 7, Savile Row, Burlington Gardens, the house in which Sheridan died in 1814. He was one of the most noticeable members of the Reform Club, though he seemed always to avoid attracting attention; an enigmatical personage, about whom little was known, except that he was a polished man of the world. People said that he resembled Byron,—at least that his head was Byronic; but he was a bearded, tranquil Byron, who might live on a thousand years without growing old.

—JULES VERNE, *Around the World in Eighty Days,*
trans. George Makepeace Towle

Studs Lonigan, on the verge of fifteen, and wearing his first suit of long trousers, stood in the bathroom with a Sweet Caporal pasted in his mug. His hands were jammed in his trouser pockets, and he sneered. He puffed, drew the fag out of his mouth, inhaled and said to himself:

Well, I'm kissin' the old dump goodbye tonight.

—JAMES T. FARRELL, *Studs Lonigan*

Alexey Fyodorovitch Karamazov was the third son of Fyodor Pavlovitch Karamazov, a landowner well known in our district in his own day, and still remembered among us owing to his gloomy and tragic death, which happened thirteen years ago, and which I shall describe in its proper place. For the present I will only say that this "landowner"—for so we used to call him, although he hardly spent a day of his life on his own estate—was a strange type, yet one pretty frequently to be met with, a type abject and vicious and at the same time senseless. But he was one of those senseless persons who are very well capable of looking after their worldly affairs, and, apparently, after nothing else.

—FYODOR DOSTOYEVSKY, *The Brothers Karamazov,*
trans. Constance Garnett

Amory Blaine inherited from his mother every trait, except the stray inexpressible few, that made him worth while. His father, an ineffectual, inarticulate man with a taste for Byron and a habit of drowsing over the *Encyclopœdia Britannica,* grew wealthy at thirty through the death of two elder brothers, successful Chicago brokers, and in the first flush of feeling that the world was his, went to Bar Harbor and met Beatrice O'Hara. In consequence, Stephen Blaine handed down to posterity his height of just under six feet and his tendency to waver at crucial moments, these two abstractions appearing in his son Amory.

—F. SCOTT FITZGERALD, *This Side of Paradise*

Samuel Spade's jaw was long and bony, his chin a jutting v under the more flexible v of his mouth. His nostrils curved back to make another, smaller, v. His yellow-grey eyes were horizontal. The *v motif* was picked up again by thickish brows rising outward from twin creases above a hooked nose,

and his pale brown hair grew down—from high flat temples—
in a point on his forehead. He looked rather pleasantly like a
blond Satan. He said to Effie Perine: "Yes, sweetheart?"
—DASHIELL HAMMETT, *The Maltese Falcon*

Mr. George Lawrence, C.M.G., First Class District Officer
of His Majesty's Civil Service, sat at the door of his tent and
viewed the African desert scene with the eye of extreme dis-
favour. There was beauty neither in the landscape nor in the
eye of the beholder.
—PERCIVAL CHRISTOPHER WREN, *Beau Geste*

Roy Hobbs pawed at the glass before thinking to prick a
match with his thumbnail and hold the spurting flame in his
cupped palm close to the lower berth window, but by then
he had figured it was a tunnel they were passing through and
was no longer surprised at the bright sight of himself holding
a yellow light over his head, peering back in.
—BERNARD MALAMUD, *The Natural*

Lov Bensey trudged homeward through the deep white sand
of the gully-washed tobacco road with a sack of winter
turnips on his back. He had put himself to a lot of trouble to
get the turnips; it was a long and tiresome walk all the way
to Fuller and back again.
—ERSKINE CALDWELL, *Tobacco Road*

Lolita, light of my life, fire of my loins. My sin, my soul. Lo-lee-ta: the tip of the tongue taking a trip of three steps down the palate to tap, at three, on the teeth. Lo. Lee. Ta.

She was Lo, plain Lo, in the morning, standing four feet ten in one sock. She was Lola in slacks. She was Dolly at school. She was Dolores on the dotted line. But in my arms she was always Lolita.

—VLADIMIR NABOKOV, *Lolita*

The Time Traveller (for so it will be convenient to speak of him) was expounding a recondite matter to us. His grey eyes shone and twinkled, and his usually pale face was flushed and animated. The fire burned brightly, and the soft radiance of the incandescent lights in the lilies of silver caught the bubbles that flashed and passed in our glasses.

—H. G. WELLS, *The Time Machine*

Gary Cooper White was born in Jersey City, New Jersey. He moved to Georgia the year he began school, when his mother's husband, number three of five, got a job in a mill there. Some of the feeling you get from the resulting combination of accents is, inevitably, lost in the transcription from the police tapes. But I've tried to note questions, interruptions and clear changes in emotion that came through in his voice.

—JUDITH ROSSNER, *Looking for Mr. Goodbar*

First page of the (apparently) complete manuscript version of H. G. Wells's *The Time Machine. (The University of Illinois at Urbana-Champaign)*

Mr. Verloc, going out in the morning, left his shop nominally in charge of his brother-in-law. It could be done, because there was very little business at any time, and practically none at all before the evening. Mr. Verloc cared but little about his ostensible business. And, moreover, his wife was in charge of his brother-in-law.

—JOSEPH CONRAD, *The Secret Agent*

*Stately, plump Buck Mulligan came from the stairhead, bearing a bowl of lather on which a mirror and a razor lay crossed. A yellow dressinggown, ungirdled, was sustained gently behind him on the mild morning air. He held the bowl aloft and intoned:
    —*Introibo ad altare Dei.*

—JAMES JOYCE, *Ulysses*

Soames Forsyte emerged from the Knightsbridge Hotel, where he was staying, in the afternoon of the 12th of May, 1920, with the intention of visiting a collection of pictures in a Gallery off Cork Street, and looking into the Future. He walked. Since the War he never took a cab if he could help it. Their drivers were, in his view, an uncivil lot, though now that the War was over and supply beginning to exceed demand again, getting more civil in accordance with the custom of human nature. Still, he had not forgiven them, deeply identifying them with gloomy memories, and now, dimly, like all members of their class, with revolution.

—JOHN GALSWORTHY, *To Let*

Old Lady Macleod was a good woman, though subject to two most serious drawbacks. She was a Calvinistic Sabbatarian in religion, and a devout believer in the high rank of her noble relatives. She could almost worship a youthful marquis, though he lived a life that would disgrace a heathen among heathens; and she could condemn crowds of commonplace men and women to eternal torments because they listened to profane music in a park on Sunday. Yet she was a good woman. She strove to love her neighbours, and lived in trust of a better world.

—ANTHONY TROLLOPE, *The Pallisers*

Mr. Utterson the lawyer was a man of a rugged countenance, that was never lighted by a smile; cold, scanty and embarrassed in discourse; backward in sentiment; lean, long, dusty, dreary, and yet somehow lovable. At friendly meetings, and when the wine was to his taste, something eminently human beaconed from his eye; something indeed which never found its way into his talk, but which spoke not only in these silent symbols of the after-dinner face, but more often and loudly in the acts of his life.

—ROBERT LOUIS STEVENSON, *The Strange Case of Dr. Jekyll and Mr. Hyde*

Hazel Motes sat at a forward angle on the green plush train seat, looking one minute at the window as if he might want to jump out of it, and the next down the aisle at the other end of the car. The train was racing through tree tops that fell away at intervals and showed the sun standing, very red, on the edge of the farthest woods.

—FLANNERY O'CONNOR, *Wise Blood*

Gumbril, Theodore Gumbril Junior, B.A. Oxon, sat in his oaken stall on the north side of the School Chapel and wondered, as he listened through the uneasy silence of half a thousand schoolboys to the First Lesson, pondered, as he looked up at the vast window opposite, all blue and jaundiced and bloody with nineteenth century glass, speculated in his rapid and rambling way about the existence and the nature of God.

—ALDOUS HUXLEY, *Antic Hay*

Ursula and Gudrun Brangwen sat one morning in the window-bay of their father's house in Beldover, working and talking. Ursula was stitching a piece of brightly-coloured embroidery, and Gudrun was drawing upon a board which she held on her knee. They were mostly silent, talking as their thoughts strayed through their minds.

"Ursula," said Gudrun, "don't you *really want* to get married?"

—D. H. LAWRENCE, *Women in Love*

One afternoon, in an early summer of this century, when Laura Rowan was just eighteen, she sat, embroidering a handkerchief, on the steps leading down from the terrace of her father's house to the gardens communally owned by the residents in Radnage Square. She liked embroidery. It was a solitary pastime and nobody bothered to interfere with it.

—REBECCA WEST, *The Birds Fall Down*

Running out of gas, Rabbit Angstrom thinks as he stands behind the summer-dusty windows of the Springer Motors display room watching the traffic go by on Route 111, traffic somehow thin and scared compared to what it used to be. The fucking world is running out of gas.

—JOHN UPDIKE, *Rabbit Is Rich*

Standing amid the tan, excited post-Christmas crowd at the Southwest Florida Regional Airport, Rabbit Angstrom has a funny sudden feeling that what he has come to meet, what's floating in unseen about to land, is not his son Nelson and daughter-in-law Pru and their two children but something more ominous and intimately his: his own death, shaped vaguely like an airplane.

—JOHN UPDIKE, *Rabbit at Rest*

Riding up the winding road of Saint Agnes Cemetery in the back of the rattling old truck, Francis Phelan became aware that the dead, even more than the living, settled down in neighborhoods. The truck was suddenly surrounded by fields of monuments and cenotaphs of kindred design and striking size, all guarding the privileged dead.

—WILLIAM KENNEDY, *Ironweed*

It was just noon that Sunday morning when the sheriff reached the jail with Lucas Beauchamp though the whole town (the whole county too for that matter) had known since the night before that Lucas had killed a white man.

He was there, waiting.

—WILLIAM FAULKNER, *Intruder in the Dust*

In the shade of the house, in the sunshine on the river bank by the boats, in the shade of the sallow wood and the fig tree, Siddhartha, the handsome Brahmin's son, grew up with his friend Govinda. The sun browned his slender shoulders on the river bank, while bathing at the holy ablutions, at the holy sacrifices. Shadows passed across his eyes in the mango grove during play, while his mother sang, during his father's teachings, when with the learned men.

—HERMANN HESSE, *Siddhartha,* trans. Hilda Rosner

In the prime assurance of his youth, in the fresh arrogance of his wisdom, and power in wisdom, with a sense of his extreme handsomeness, if not indeed beauty (for Gerta had said more than once that he was beautiful, and his own mirror had pleasantly corroborated this) Jasper Ammen leaned

from the sixth floor window and projected his own image
upon the world. In particular, he projected it against the
sunset: a more melancholy, and therefore more pleasant,
form of this occupation, and one in which he frequently
indulged.

—CONRAD AIKEN, *King Coffin*

The book of ballads published by Von Humboldt Fleisher in
the Thirties was an immediate hit. Humboldt was just what
everyone had been waiting for. Out in the Midwest I had
certainly been waiting eagerly, I can tell you that. An avant-
garde writer, the first of a new generation, he was handsome,
fair, large, serious, witty, he was learned. The guy had it all.

—SAUL BELLOW, *Humboldt's Gift*

Although she herself was ill enough to justify being in bed
had she been a person weakminded enough to give up, Rose
Sayer could see that her brother, the Reverend Samuel Sayer,
was far more ill. He was very, very weak indeed, and when
he knelt to offer up the evening prayer the movement was
more like an involuntary collapse than a purposed gesture,
and the hands which he raised trembled violently. Rose
could see, in the moment before she devoutly closed her
eyes, how thin and transparent those hands were, and how
the bones of the wrists could be seen with almost the defini-
tion of a skeleton's.

—C. S. FORESTER, *The African Queen*

The little boy named Ulysses Macauley one day stood over the new gopher hole in the backyard of his house on Santa Clara Avenue in Ithaca, California. The gopher of this hole pushed up fresh moist dirt and peeked out at the boy, who was certainly a stranger but perhaps not an enemy.

—WILLIAM SAROYAN, *The Human Comedy*

When Farmer Oak smiled, the corners of his mouth spread till they were within an unimportant distance of his ears, his eyes were reduced to mere chinks, and diverging wrinkles appeared round them, extending upon his countenance like the rays in a rudimentary sketch of the rising sun.

His Christian name was Gabriel, and on working days he was a young man of sound judgment, easy motions, proper dress, and general good character. On Sundays he was a man of misty views, rather given to postponing, and hampered by his best clothes and unbrella: upon the whole, one who felt himself to occupy morally that vast middle space of Laodicean neutrality which lay between the Communion people of the parish and the drunken section,—that is, he went to church, but yawned privately by the time the congregation reached the Nicene creed, and thought of what there would be for dinner when he meant to be listening to the sermon.

—THOMAS HARDY, *Far from the Madding Crowd*

On December 8th, 1915, Meggie Cleary had her fourth birthday. After the breakfast dishes were put away her mother

silently thrust a brown paper parcel into her arms and
ordered her outside. So Meggie squatted down behind the
gorse bush next to the front gate and tugged impatiently.
Her fingers were clumsy, the wrapping heavy; it smelled
faintly of the Wahine general store, which told her that
whatever lay inside the parcel had miraculously been *bought,*
not homemade or donated.

—COLLEEN MCCULLOCH, *The Thorn Birds*

No one who had ever seen Catherine Morland in her infancy would have supposed her born to be an heroine. Her situation in life, the character of her father and mother, her own
person and disposition, were all equally against her.

—JANE AUSTEN, *Northanger Abbey*

She waited, Kate Croy, for her father to come in, but he
kept her unconscionably, and there were moments at which
she showed herself, in the glass over the mantel, a face posi-
tively pale with the irritation that had brought her to the
point of going away without sight of him. It was at this
point, however, that she remained; changing her place, moving from the shabby sofa to the armchair upholstered in a
glazed cloth that gave at once—she had tried it—the sense of
the slippery and of the sticky.

—HENRY JAMES, *The Wings of the Dove*

At forty-one, Elizabeth Aidallbery had a way of dwelling on her past, and when memories were doubtful there were photographs to help her. At two she was anonymous on a tartan rug. At five she was freckled, thin-legged and laughing in a striped dress. At ten she was sunburnt beneath a tree, her pale hair in plaits, standing with Henry in the garden where her own children played now. There was a wedding photograph, an image that revealed the faded blueness of her eyes because it was in colour.

—WILLIAM TREVOR, *Elizabeth Alone*

Her first name was India—she was never able to get used to it. It seemed to her that her parents must have been thinking of someone else when they named her. Or were they hoping for another sort of daughter? As a child she was often on the point of inquiring, but time passed, and she never did.

—EVAN S. CONNELL, *Mrs. Bridge*

Bizarre as was the name she bore, Kim Ravenal always said she was thankful it had been no worse. She knew whereof she spoke, for it was literally by a breath that she had escaped being called Mississippi.

"Imagine Mississippi Ravenal!" she often said, in later years. "They'd have cut it to Missy, I suppose, or even Sippy, if you can bear to think of anything so horrible. And then I'd have had to change my name or give up the stage altogether.

Because who'd go to see—seriously, I mean—an actress named Sippy? It sounds half-witted, for some reason. Kim's bad enough, God knows."

—EDNA FERBER, *Show Boat*

Ellerbee had been having a bad time of it. He'd had financial reversals. Change would slip out of his pockets and slide down into the crevices of other people's furniture. He dropped deposit bottles and lost money in pay phones and vending machines. He overtipped in dark taxicabs. He had many such financial reversals.

—STANLEY ELKIN, *The Living End*

My Uncle Daniel's just like your uncle, if you've got one—only he has one weakness. He loves society and he gets carried away. If he hears our voices, he'll come right down those stairs, supper ready or no. When he sees you sitting in the lobby of the Beulah, he'll take the other end of the sofa and then move closer up to see what you've got to say for yourself; and then he's liable to give you a little hug and start trying to give you something.

—EUDORA WELTY, *The Ponder Heart*

Mr. Tench went out to look for his ether cylinder: out into the blazing Mexican sun and the bleaching dust. A few buzzards looked down from the roof with shabby indifference: he wasn't carrion yet. A faint feeling of rebellion stirred in Mr. Tench's heart, and he wrenched up a piece of the road with splintering finger-nails and tossed it feebly up at them.

—GRAHAM GREENE, *The Power and the Glory*

5 ✿ THE IMPERSONAL PRONOUN

elying on only the personal pronoun to introduce a character is like dropping a scrim curtain
in front of a scene on the stage: we see the action
perfectly well, but the identity of the faces is hidden from us until the stage manager permits the curtain to
rise. The effect is also the same: an enhanced sense of drama
and mystery: "He awoke, opened his eyes. The room meant
very little to him; he was too deeply immersed in the non-
being from which he had just come" (Paul Bowles, *The Sheltering Sky*).

Witholding the name of a character who begins a book,
whether principal or subordinate, gained popularity as the
novel moved into the twentieth century. Beginning a novel
with "he" or "she" allowed the author to involve the reader
in a description or action of the character without the somewhat artificial, self-conscious use of the proper name. It

especially suited the short-sentenced, blunt style of writers like Hemingway, although it had of course been used effectively by authors like Conrad—in *Lord Jim,* and Kipling—in *Kim.* In expert hands like these, the technique was dramatic, powerful, almost poetic.

Impersonally Speaking ⁓
We learn where and what the character is, before we learn who he or she is.

He lay flat on the brown, pine-needled floor of the forest, his chin on his folded arms, and high overhead the wind blew in the tops of the pine trees. The mountainside sloped gently where he lay; but below it was steep and he could see the dark of the oiled road winding through the pass. There was a stream alongside the road and far down the pass he saw a mill beside the stream and the falling water of the dam, white in the summer sunlight.

—ERNEST HEMINGWAY, *For Whom the Bell Tolls*

He was an inch, perhaps two, under six feet, powerfully built, and he advanced straight at you with a slight stoop of the shoulders, head forward, and a fixed from-under stare which made you think of a charging bull. His voice was deep, loud, and his manner displayed a kind of dogged self-assertion which had nothing aggressive in it. It seemed a necessity, and it was directed apparently as much at himself as at anybody else. He was spotlessly neat, apparelled in immaculate white from shoes to hat, and in the various Eastern ports where he got his living as ship-chandler's water-clerk he was very popular.

—JOSEPH CONRAD, *Lord Jim*

She was so deeply imbedded in my consciousness that for the first year of school I seem to have believed that each of my teachers was my mother in disguise. As soon as the last bell had sounded, I would rush off for home, wondering as I ran if I could possibly make it to our apartment before she had succeeded in transforming herself. Invariably she was already in the kitchen by the time I arrived, and setting out my milk and cookies.

—PHILIP ROTH, *Portnoy's Complaint*

He rode into our valley in the summer of '89. I was a kid then, barely topping the backboard of father's old chuckwagon. I was on the upper rail of our small corral, soaking in the late afternoon sun, when I saw him far down the road where it swung into the valley from the open plain beyond.

—JACK SCHAEFER, *Shane*

Often he thought: My life did not begin until I knew her.
  She would like to hear this, he was sure, but he did not

know how to tell her. In the extremity of passion he cried out in a frantic voice: "I love you!" yet even these words were unsatisfactory.

—EVAN S. CONNELL, *Mr. Bridge*

When she was home from her boarding-school I used to see her almost every day sometimes, because their house was right opposite the Town Hall Annexe. She and her younger sister used to go in and out a lot, often with young men, which of course I didn't like. When I had a free moment from the files and ledgers I stood by the window and used to look down over the road over the frosting and sometimes I'd see her. In the evening I marked it in my observations diary, at first with X, and then when I knew her name with M.

—JOHN FOWLES, *The Collector*

As a junior of exceptional promise, he had been sent to Egypt for a year in order to improve his Arabic and found himself attached to the High Commission as a sort of scribe to await his first diplomatic posting; but he was already conducting himself as a young secretary of legation, fully aware of the responsibilities of future office. Only somehow today it was rather more difficult than usual to be reserved, so exciting had the fish-drive become.

—LAWRENCE DURRELL, *Mountolive*

A bird cried out on the roof, and he woke up. It was the middle of the afternoon, in the heat, in Africa; he knew at once where he was. Not even in the suspended seconds between sleep and waking was he left behind in the house in Wiltshire, lying, now, deep in the snow of a hard winter.

—NADINE GORDIMER, *A Guest of Honour*

He awoke, opened his eyes. The room meant very little to him; he was too deeply immersed in the non-being from which he had just come. If he had not the energy to ascertain his position in time and space, he also lacked the desire. He was somewhere, he had come back through vast regions from nowhere; there was the certitude of an infinite sadness at the core of his consciousness, but the sadness was reassuring, because it alone was familiar.

—PAUL BOWLES, *The Sheltering Sky*

He sat before the mirror of the second-floor bedroom sketching his lean cheeks with their high bone ridges, the flat broad forehead, and ears too far back on the head, the dark hair curling forward in thatches, the amber-colored eyes wide-set but heavy-lidded.

"I'm not well designed," thought the thirteen-year-old with serious concentration.

—IRVING STONE, *The Agony and the Ecstasy*

He sat, in defiance of municipal orders, astride the gun Zam-Zammah on her brick platform opposite the old Ajaib-Gher—the Wonder House, as the natives called the Lahore Museum. Who hold Zam-Zammah, that 'fire-breathing dragon,' hold the Punjab; for the great green-bronze piece is always first of the conqueror's loot.

—RUDYARD KIPLING, *Kim*

He was born with a gift of laughter and a sense that the world was mad. And that was all his patrimony. His very paternity was obscure, although the village of Gavrillac had long since dispelled the cloud of mystery that hung about it. Those simple Brittany folk were not so simple as to be deceived by a pretended relationship which did not even possess the virtue of originality. When a nobleman, for no apparent reason, announces himself the godfather of an infant fetched no man knew whence, and thereafter cares for the lad's rearing and education, the most unsophisticated of country folk perfectly understand the situation.

—RAFAEL SABATINI, *Scaramouche*

He was an old man who fished alone in a skiff in the Gulf Stream and he had gone eighty-four days now without taking a fish. In the first forty days a boy had been with him. But after forty days without a fish the boy's parents had told him that the old man was now definitely and finally *salao,* which is the worst form of unlucky, and the boy had gone at their orders in another boat which caught three good fish the first week. It made the boy sad to see the old man come in each day with his skiff empty and he always went down to help him carry either the coiled lines or the gaff and harpoon and the sail that was furled around the mast. The sail was patched with flour sacks and, furled, it looked like the flag of permanent defeat.

—ERNEST HEMINGWAY, *The Old Man and the Sea*

When he finished packing, he walked out on to the third-floor porch of the barracks brushing the dust from his hands, a very neat and deceptively slim young man in the summer khakis that were still early morning fresh.

He leaned his elbows on the porch ledge and stood looking down through the screens at the familiar scene of the barracks square laid out below with the tiers of porches dark in the faces of the three-story concrete barracks fronting on the square. He was feeling a half-sheepish affection for his vantage point that he was leaving.

—JAMES JONES, *From Here to Eternity*

I believe he had seen us out of the window coming off to dine in the dinghy of a fourteen-ton yawl belonging to Marlow, my host and skipper. We helped the boy we had with us to haul the boat up on the landing-stage before we went up to the river-side inn, where we found our new acquaintance eating his dinner in dignified loneliness at the head of a long table, white and inhospitable like a snow bank.

—JOSEPH CONRAD, *Chance*

Chance

A tale with comments

Chance

~~A ship-board tale.~~

by

Joseph Conrad

2 Copies please

— Did any of you gentlemen know
Powell, he began and paused to light
his pipe, looking at us fixedly the
while. His eyes sparkling ~~behind the light~~
~~flame of the match~~ ~~grew austere with~~
~~disappointment~~ with the intoxication
of a reminiscence coming up from
the depths of memory, like generous
wine from the darkness ~~cold~~ of a ~~warm~~ cellar,
grew austere with disappointment
at our silence and immobility in
the gathering dusk of the low
room. "What? Not Archie Powell?
Then I see that none of you had
ever earned his bread at sea—out
of this port of London at any
rate. You ~~are~~ but yachtsmen
~~after all ...~~

The first two pages of the original manuscript of Joseph Conrad's *Chance*. Conrad later began the story's action on page 2. *(Henry W. and Albert A. Berg Collection, The New York Public Library, Astor, Lenox and Tilden Foundations)*

altogether in the dingey of
that yawl yonder and when
eating my solitary dinner

after all" -

He had been in a crowd of four overloading come off
in the dingey of the
"Nellie" the 14th yawl belonging to our friend
and skipper who with his usual
good nature was himself pulling
us ashore. But we all helped
zealously to haul up the boat up on the stage
(a work a boy could have done
singlehanded) before we went
up to the riverside inn where we
found our new acquaintance
eating his solitary dinner in a
sort of dignified loneliness
at the head of vast table white
and cool like a snowfield —

In hidden vainglory he had vowed that he would stay awake straight through the night, for he had wondered, and not without scorn, how they, grown men, could give way to sleep on this night of all the nights in their life, leaving Him without one friend in His worst hour; but some while before midnight, still unaware that he was so much as drowsy, he had fallen asleep; and now this listening sleep was broken and instantly Richard lay sharp awake, aware of his failure and of the night.

—JAMES AGEE, *The Morning Watch*

6 ❧ SETTING THE SETTING

ew elements of the novel perform as many useful and important functions as the setting. The setting lifts us out of the world we know to a different time and place so that we can experience a period, a culture, a country that might be completely alien to us. It sets the stage for the drama that is to unfold, and prepares us to understand why a character acts the way he does. It can create a mood so strong that it almost becomes another character in the story, pushing the hero helplessly to his fate, or challenging him to struggle against it. It can be a symbol of the hero's strength, as Tara is to Scarlett O'Hara in *Gone With the Wind*. Even if the setting is unobtrusive or ordinary, as it is in many contemporary novels like those of Ann Beattie and John Updike, it can make a point by emphasizing the banality of that everyday life. No matter what its function, however, the novel must have a setting; it is up to the author to decide what use he wishes to make of it.

When the setting begins a book, it assumes a dramatic prominence, emphasizing the importance to the author of the geographic or cultural or atmospheric elements that will influence the action. When John Steinbeck begins, "The Salinas Valley is in Northern California," he sets the boundaries for the characters of *East of Eden*. When Henry James writes in *The American,* "On a brilliant day in May, in the year 1868, a gentleman was reclining at his ease on the great circular divan which at that period occupied the centre of the Salon Carré, in the Museum of the Louvre," he indicates not just a time in space, but the cultural ambiance we are to expect. When Thomas Hardy relates, "A Saturday afternoon in November was approaching the time of twilight, and the vast tract of unenclosed wild known as Egdon Heath embrowned itself moment by moment," he is introducing a landscape that is to be an omnipresent force in *The Return of the Native.*

For Hardy, the dark heaths, the wild, high-cliffed coastline, the hedge-rowed farmland, the clustered thatch-roofed cottages of England's West Country provided all three of these important functions of the setting; in his novels he seldom needed to stray far from home. So, too, William Faulkner, Sarah Orne Jewett, and D. H. Lawrence give us, in novel after novel, detailed glimpses into the South, the New England town, the north of England. Sometimes a fictional name thinly masks an actual location, like Hardy's Wessex, or Faulkner's Yoknapatawpha County, but the reality of the setting shines through clearly, placing and influencing the characters, and convincing us that we are there.

The selections in this chapter illustrate the three major elements of setting: Geography, Time, and Weather. The first, although it may appear to be nothing more than description, is actually giving us vital information, directly or indirectly, about the location that will be central to the story. "Except for the Marabar Caves ..." begins Forster's *A Passage to India,* quickly passing by us what we will discover to be the focus of the novel. The second is preparing us to enter a particular place at a particular time. "While the present century was in its teens, and on one sunshiny morning in June, there drove up to the great iron gate of Miss Pinkerton's academy for young ladies, on Chiswick Mall, a large family coach ..." writes Thackeray in *Vanity Fair.* We abandon the present to travel with the author backward, or in the case of authors like H. G. Wells, forward, in space. The last, the element of Weather, provides the atmosphere and the mood of the story or the principal character. "The cold passed reluctantly from the earth, and the retiring fogs revealed an army stretched out on the hills, resting," opens Stephen Crane's *The Red Badge of Courage,* painting a gray setting for his episode of the Civil War.

The Scene Is Set ⌁
The author places the story geographically.

Except for the Marabar Caves—and they are twenty miles off—the city of Chandrapore presents nothing extraordinary. Edged rather than washed by the River Ganges, it trails for a couple of miles along the bank, scarcely distinguishable from the rubbish it deposits so freely. There are no bathing-steps on the river front, as the Ganges happens not to be holy here; indeed there is no river front, and bazaars shut out the wide and shifting panorama of the stream. The streets are mean, the temples ineffective, and though a few fine houses exist they are hidden away in gardens or down alleys whose filth deters all but the invited guest.

—E. M. FORSTER, *A Passage to India*

On the pleasant shore of the French Riviera, about half way between Marseilles and the Italian border, stands a large, proud, rose-colored hotel. Deferential palms cool its flushed façade, and before it stretches a short dazzling beach. Lately it has become a summer resort of notable and fashionable people; a decade ago it was almost deserted after its English clientele went north in April.

—F. SCOTT FITZGERALD, *Tender Is the Night*

The rambler who, for old association's sake, should trace the forsaken coach-road running almost in a meridional line from Bristol to the south shore of England, would find himself during the latter half of his journey in the vicinity of some extensive woodlands, interspersed with apple-orchards. Here the trees, timber or fruit-bearing as the case may be, make the wayside hedges ragged by their drip and shade, their lower limbs stretching in level repose over the road, as though reclining on the insubstantial air. At one place, on the skirts of Blackmoor Vale, where the bold brow of High-Stoy Hill is seen two or three miles ahead, the leaves lie so thick in autumn as to completely bury the track. The spot is lonely, and when the days are darkening the many gay charioteers now perished who have rolled along the way, the blistered soles that have trodden it, and the tears that have wetted it, return upon the mind of the loiterer.

—THOMAS HARDY, *The Woodlanders*

Not very far from Upton-on-Severn—between it, in fact, and the Malvern Hills—stands the country seat of the Gordons of Bramley; well-timbered, well-cottaged, well-fenced and well-watered, having, in this latter respect, a stream that forks in exactly the right position to feed two large lakes in the grounds.

The House itself is of Georgian red brick, with charming circular windows near the roof. It has dignity and pride without ostentation, self-assurance without arrogance, repose without inertia; and a gentle aloofness that, to those who know its spirit, but adds to its value as a home. It is indeed like certain lovely women who, now old, belong to a bygone generation—women who in youth were passionate but seemly; difficult to win but when won, all-fulfilling.

—RADCLYFFE HALL, *The Well of Loneliness*

The suburb of Saffron Park lay on the sunset side of London, as red and ragged as a cloud of sunset. It was built of a bright brick throughout; its skyline was fantastic, and even its ground plan was wild. It had been the outburst of a speculative builder, faintly tinged with art, who called its architecture sometimes Elizabethan and sometimes Queen Anne, apparently under the impression that the two sovereigns were identical.

—G. K. CHESTERTON, *The Man Who Was Thursday*

riverrun, past Eve and Adam's, from swerve of shore to bend of bay, brings us by a commodius vicus of recirculation back to Howth Castle and Environs.

Sir Tristam, violer d'amores, fr'over the short sea, had passencore rearrived from North Armorica on this side the scraggy isthmus of Europe Minor to wielderfight his penisolate war: nor had topsawyer's rocks by the stream Oconee exaggerated themselse to Laurens County's gorgios while they went doublin their mumper all the time: nor avoice from afire bellowsed mishe mishe to tauftauf thuartpeatrick: not yet, though venissoon after, had a kidscad buttended a bland old isaac: not yet, though all's fair in vanessy, were sosie sesthers wroth with twone nathandjoe.

—JAMES JOYCE, *Finnegan's Wake*

"The Bottoms" succeeded to "Hell Row." Hell Row was a block of thatched, bulging cottages that stood by the brook-

side on Greenhill Lane. There lived the colliers who worked
in the little gin-pits two fields away. The brook ran under the
alder trees, scarcely soiled by these small mines, whose coal
was drawn to the surface by donkeys that plodded wearily in
a circle round a gin. And all over the countryside were these
same pits, some of which had been worked in the time of
Charles II, the few colliers and the donkeys burrowing down
like ants into the earth, making queer mounds and little
black places among the corn-fields and the meadows. And
the cottages of these coal-miners, in blocks and pairs here
and there, together with odd farms and homes of the
stockingers, straying over the parish, formed the village of
Bestwood.

—D. H. LAWRENCE, *Sons and Lovers*

The small town of Verrières may be regarded as one of the
most attractive in the Franche-Compté. Its white houses
with their high pitched roofs of red tiles are spread over the
slope of a hill, the slightest contours of which are indicated
by clumps of sturdy chestnuts. The Doubs runs some hundreds of feet below its fortifications, built in times past by the
Spaniards, and now in ruins.

—STENDHAL, *The Red and the Black,*
trans. C. K. Scott Moncrieff

Half-way down a by-street of one of our New England
towns stands a rusty wooden house, with seven acutely

peaked gables, facing towards various points of the compass, and a huge, clustered chimney in the midst. The street is Pyncheon Street; the house is the old Pyncheon House; and an elm-tree, of wide circumference, rooted before the door, is familiar to every town-born child by the title of the Pyncheon Elm. On my occasional visits to the town aforesaid, I seldom failed to turn down Pyncheon Street, for the sake of passing through the shadow of these two antiquities,—the great elm-tree and the weather-beaten edifice.

—NATHANIEL HAWTHORNE, *The House of the Seven Gables*

At the end of the rue Guénégaud, as you come up from the river, you find the Passage du Pont-Neuf, a sort of narrow, dark corridor connecting rue Mazarine and rue de Seine. This passage is thirty yards long and two in width at the most; it is paved with yellowish flagstones, worn and loose, which always exude a damp, pungent smell, and it is covered with a flat, glazed roofing black with grime.

On fine summer days, when the streets are baking in the oppressive heat, a whitish light does fall through the dingy glass roofing and hang dismally about this arcade, but on nasty winter ones, on foggy mornings, the panes send down nothing but gloom on to the greasy pavement below, and dirty, evil gloom at that.

—ÉMILE ZOLA, *Thérèse Raquin,* trans. Leonard Tancock

The towers of Zenith aspired above the morning mist; austere towers of steel and cement and limestone, sturdy as cliffs and delicate as silver rods. They were neither citadels nor churches, but frankly and beautifully office-buildings.

The mist took pity on the fretted structures of earlier generations: the Post Office with its shingle-tortured mansard, the red brick minarets of hulking old houses, factories with stingy and sooted windows, wooden tenements colored like mud. The city was full of such grotesqueries, but the clean towers were thrusting them from the business center, and on the farther hills were shining new houses, homes—they seemed—for laughter and tranquillity.

—SINCLAIR LEWIS, *Babbitt*

Two elderly women sat knitting on that part of the verandah which was screened from the sun by a golden shower creeper; the tough stems were so thick with flower it was as if the glaring afternoon was dammed against them in a surf of its own light made visible in the dripping, orange-coloured clusters. Inside this coloured barrier was a darkened recess, rough mud walls (the outer walls of the house itself) forming two sides, the third consisting of a bench loaded with painted petrol tins which held pink and white geraniums. The sun splashed liberal gold through the foliage, over the red cement floor, and over the ladies. They had been here since lunchtime, and would remain until sunset, talking, talking incessantly, their tongues mercifully let off the leash. They

were Mrs. Quest and Mrs. Van Rensberg; and Martha
Quest, a girl of fifteen, sat on the steps in full sunshine,
clumsily twisting herself to keep the glare from her book
with her own shadow.

—DORIS LESSING, *Martha Quest*

Now the shadow of the column—the column which sup-
ports the southwest corner of the roof—divides the corre-
sponding corner of the veranda into two equal parts. This
veranda is a wide, covered gallery surrounding the house on
three sides. Since its width is the same for the central portion
as for the sides, the line of shadow cast by the column
extends precisely to the corner of the house; but it stops
there, for only the veranda flagstones are reached by the sun,
which is still too high in the sky. The wooden walls of the
house—that is, its front and west gable-end—are still protect-
ed from the sun by the roof (common to the house proper
and the terrace). So at this moment the shadow of the outer
edge of the roof coincides exactly with the right angle
formed by the terrace and the two vertical surfaces of the
corner of the house.

—ALAIN ROBBE-GRILLET, *Jealousy*, trans. Richard Howard

Paint me a small railroad station then, ten minutes before
dark. Beyond the platform are the waters of the Wekonsett
River, reflecting a somber afterglow. The architecture of the

station is oddly informal, gloomy but unserious, and mostly resembles a pergola, cottage or summer house although this is a climate of harsh winters. The lamps along the platform burn with a nearly palpable plaintiveness. The setting seems in some way to be at the heart of the matter.

—JOHN CHEEVER, *Bullet Park*

Imagine, then, a flat landscape, dark for the moment, but even so conveying to a girl running in the still deeper shadow cast by the wall of the Bibighar Gardens an idea of immensity, of distance, such as years before Miss Crane had been conscious of standing where a lane ended and cultivation began: a different landscape but also in the alluvial plain between the mountains of the north and the plateau of the south.

It is a landscape which a few hours ago, between the rainfall and the short twilight, extracted colour from the spectrum of the setting sun and dyed every one of its own surfaces that could absorb light: the ochre walls of the houses in the old town (which are stained too with their bloody past and uneasy present); the moving water of the river and the still water of the tanks; the shiny stubble, the ploughed earth, of distant fields; the metal of the grand trunk road. In this landscape trees are sparse, except among the white bungalows of the civil lines. On the horizon there is a violet smudge of hill country.

—PAUL SCOTT, *The Jewel in the Crown*

There is a lovely road that runs from Ixopo into the hills. These hills are grass-covered and rolling, and they are lovely beyond any singing of it. The road climbs seven miles into them, to Carisbrooke; and from there, if there is no mist, you look down on one of the fairest valleys of Africa. About you there is grass and bracken and you may hear the forlorn crying of the titihoya, one of the birds of the veld. Below you is the valley of the Umzimkulu, on its journey from the Drakensberg to the sea; and beyond and behind the river, great hill after great hill; and beyond and behind them, the mountains of Ingeli and East Griqualand.

—ALAN PATON, *Cry, the Beloved Country*

MASON CITY.

To get there you follow Highway 58, going northeast out of the city, and it is a good highway and new. Or was new, that day we went up it. You look up the highway and it is straight for miles, coming at you, with the black line down the center coming at and at you, black and slick and tarry-shining against the white of the slab, and the heat dazzles up from the white slab so that only the black line is clear, coming at you with the whine of the tires, and if you don't quit staring at that line and don't take a few deep breaths and slap yourself hard on the back of the neck you'll hypnotize yourself and you'll come to just at the moment when the right front wheel hooks over into the black dirt shoulder off the slab, and you'll try to jerk her back on but you can't because the slab is high like a curb, and maybe you'll try to reach to turn

off the ignition just as she starts the dive. But you won't
make it, of course.

—ROBERT PENN WARREN, *All the King's Men*

The Salinas Valley is in Northern California. It is a long nar-
row swale between two ranges of mountains, and the Salinas
River winds and twists up the center until it falls at last into
Monterey Bay.

—JOHN STEINBECK, *East of Eden*

A few miles south of Soledad, the Salinas River drops in
close to the hillside bank and runs deep and green. The
water is warm too, for it has slipped twinkling over the yellow sands in the sunlight before reaching the narrow pool.
On one side of the river the golden foothill slopes curve up
to the strong and rocky Gabilan mountains, but on the valley
side the water is lined with trees—willows fresh and green
with every spring, carrying in their lower leaf junctures the
debris of the winter's flooding; and sycamores with mottled,
white, recumbent limbs and branches that arch over the
pool.

—JOHN STEINBECK, *Of Mice and Men*

Those two girls, Constance and Sophia Baines, paid no heed
to the manifold interest of their situation, of which, indeed,
they had never been conscious. They were, for example,

established almost precisely on the fifty-third parallel of latitude. A little way to the north of them, in the creases of a hill famous for its religious orgies, rose the river Trent, the calm and characteristic stream of middle England. Somewhat farther northwards, in the near neighbourhood of the highest public-house in the realm, rose two lesser rivers, the Dane and the Dove, which, quarrelling in early infancy, turned their back on each other, and, the one by favour of the Weaver and the other by favour of the Trent, watered between them the whole width of England, and poured themselves respectively into the Irish Sea and the German Ocean.

—ARNOLD BENNETT, *The Old Wives' Tale*

Two mountain chains traverse the republic roughly from north to south, forming between them a number of valleys and plateaus. Overlooking one of these valleys, which is dominated by two volcanoes, lies, six thousand feet above sea level, the town of Quauhnahuac. It is situated well south of the Tropic of Cancer, to be exact on the nineteenth parallel, in about the same latitude as the Revillagigedo Islands to the west in the Pacific, or very much further west, the southernmost tip of Hawaii—and as the port of Tzucox to the east on the Atlantic seaboard of Yucatan near the border of British Honduras, or very much further east, the town of Juggernaut, in India, on the Bay of Bengal.

—MALCOLM LOWRY, *Under the Volcano*

There, far below, is the knobbly backbone of England, the Pennine Range. At first, the whole dark length of it, from the Peak to Cross Fell, is visible. Then the Derbyshire hills and the Cumberland fells disappear, for you are descending, somewhere about the middle of the range, where the high moorland thrusts itself between the woollen mills of Yorkshire and the cotton mills of Lancashire. Great winds blow over miles and miles of ling and bog and black rock, and the curlews still go crying in that empty air as they did before the Romans came.

—J. B. PRIESTLEY, *The Good Companions*

A deep red glow flushed the fronts of marble palaces piled up on the slope of an arid mountain whose barren ridge traced high on the darkening sky a ghostly and glimmering outline. The winter sun was setting over the Gulf of Genoa. Behind the massive shore the sky to the east was like darkening glass. The open water too had a glassy look with a purple sheen in which the evening light lingered as if clinging to the water.

—JOSEPH CONRAD, *Suspense*

The first thing I noticed was the clarity of the air, and then the sharp green colour of the land. There was no softness anywhere. The distant hills did not blend into the sky but stood out like rocks, so close that I could almost touch them, their proximity giving me that shock of surprise and wonder

which a child feels looking for the first time through a tele-
scope. Nearer to me, too, each object had the same hard
quality, the very grass turning to single blades, springing
from a younger, harsher soil than the soil I knew.
                        —DAPHNE DU MAURIER, *The House on the Strand*

LANDSCAPE-TONES: brown to bronze, steep skyline, low
cloud, pearl ground with shadowed oyster and violet reflec-
tions. The lion-dust of desert: prophets' tombs turned to
zinc and copper at sunset on the ancient lake. Its huge sand-
faults like watermarks from the air; green and citron giving
to gunmetal, to a single plum-dark sail, moist, palpitant:
sticky-winged nymph. Taposiris is dead among its tumbling
columns and seamarks, vanished the Harpoon Men ...
Mareotis under a sky of hot lilac.
                        —LAWRENCE DURRELL, *Balthazar*

A wide plain, where the broadening Floss hurries on
between its green banks to the sea, and the loving tide, rushing to meet it, checks its passage with an impetuous embrace.
On this mighty tide the black ships—laden with the fresh-
scented fir-planks, with rounded sacks of oil-bearing seed, or
with the dark glitter of coal—are borne along to the town of
St Ogg's, which shows its aged, fluted red roofs and the broad
gables of its wharves between the low wooded hill and the
river brink, tinging the water with a soft purple hue under
the transient glance of this February sun.
                        —GEORGE ELIOT, *The Mill on the Floss*

Unearthly humps of land curved into the darkening sky like the backs of browsing pigs, like the rumps of elephants. At night when the stars rose over them they looked like a starlit herd of divine pigs. The villagers called them Hullocks.

The valleys were full of soft and windblown vegetation. The sea rolled at the foot of all as though God had brought his herd down to water.

—ENID BAGNOLD, *National Velvet*

The Jebel es Zubleh is a mountain fifty miles and more in length, and so narrow that its tracery on the map gives it a likeness to a caterpillar crawling from the south to the north. Standing on its red-and-white cliffs, and looking off under the path of the rising sun, one sees only the Desert of Arabia, where the east winds, so hateful to the vinegrowers of Jericho, have kept their playgrounds since the beginning. Its feet are well covered by sands tossed from the Euphrates, there to lie; for the mountain is a wall to the pasture-lands of Moab and Ammon on the west—lands which else had been of the desert a part.

—LEW WALLACE, *Ben-Hur*

Shy flocks of small banana-green parrots had begun to come back to the pipal trees about the bombed pagoda. But across the rice fields, scorched and barren now from the long dry season, only a few white egrets stepped daintily like ghostly cranes about the yellow dust in the heat haze. Nothing else

moved across the great plain where for three years no rice
had grown.

—H. E. BATES, *The Purple Plain*

A column of smoke rose thin and straight from the cabin
chimney. The smoke was blue where it left the red of
the clay. It trailed into the blue of the April sky and was
no longer blue but gray. The boy Jody watched it, speculating.

—MARJORIE KINNAN RAWLINGS, *The Yearling*

Time and Time Again ~
The writer takes us to a specific time and place.

While the present century was in its teens, and on one sunshiny morning in June, there drove up to the great iron gate
of Miss Pinkerton's academy for young ladies, on Chiswick
Mall, a large family coach, with two fat horses in blazing
harness, driven by a fat coachman in a three-cornered hat
and wig, at the rate of four miles an hour.

—WILLIAM MAKEPEACE THACKERAY, *Vanity Fair*

The year 1866 was signalised by a remarkable incident, a
mysterious and inexplicable phenomenon, which doubtless
no one has yet forgotten. Not to mention rumours which
agitated the maritime population, and excited the public

mind, even in the interior of continents, seafaring men were
particularly excited.

　　　—JULES VERNE, *Twenty Thousand Leagues Under the Sea*

On Friday noon, July the twentieth, 1714, the finest bridge
in all Peru broke and precipitated five travellers into the gulf
below. This bridge was on the high-road between Lima and
Cuzco and hundreds of persons passed over it every day. It
had been woven of osier by the Incas more than a century
before and visitors to the city were always led out to see it. It
was a mere ladder of thin slats swung out over the gorge,
with hand-rails of dried vine.

　　　—THORNTON WILDER, *The Bridge of San Luis Rey*

It is cold at 6:40 in the morning of a March day in Paris, and
seems even colder when a man is about to be executed by
firing squad. At that hour on March 11, 1963, in the main
courtyard of the Fort d'Ivry a French Air Force colonel
stood before a stake driven into the chilly gravel as his hands
were bound behind the post, and stared with slowly diminish-
ing disbelief at the squad of soldiers facing him twenty
metres away.

　　　—FREDERICK FORSYTH, *The Day of the Jackal*

No one would have believed in the last years of the nineteenth century that this world was being watched keenly and

closely by intelligences greater than man's and yet as mortal as his own; that as men busied themselves about their various concerns they were scrutinised and studied, perhaps almost as narrowly as a man with a microscope might scrutinise the transient creatures that swarm and multiply in a drop of water. With infinite complacency men went to and fro over this globe about their little affairs, serene in their assurance of their empire over matter.

—H. G. WELLS, *The War of the Worlds*

It was June, 1933, one week after Commencement, when Kay Leiland Strong, Vassar '33, the first of her class to run around the table at the Class Day dinner, was married to Harald Petersen, Reed '27, in the chapel of St. George's Church, P.E., Karl F. Reiland, Rector. Outside, on Stuyvesant Square, the trees were in full leaf, and the wedding guests arriving by twos and threes in taxis heard the voices of children playing round the statue of Peter Stuyvesant in the park.

—MARY MCCARTHY, *The Group*

Three hundred and forty-eight years, six months and nineteen days ago today, the people of Paris awoke to hear all the churchbells in the triple enclosure of the City, the University and the Town in full voice.

Not that 6 January 1482 is a day of which history has kept any record. There was nothing noteworthy about the event that had set the burgesses and bells of Paris in motion from early morning.

—VICTOR HUGO, *Notre-Dame of Paris,* trans. John Sturrock

In the year 1815 Monseigneur Charles-François-Bienvenu Myriel was Bishop of Digne. He was then about seventy-five, having held the bishopric since 1806.

Although it has no direct bearing on the tale we have to tell, we must nevertheless give some account of the rumours and gossip concerning him which were in circulation when he came to occupy the diocese.

—VICTOR HUGO, *Les Misérables,* trans. Norman Denny

At the striking of noon on a certain fifth of March, there occurred within a causal radius of Brandon railway station and yet beyond the deepest pools of emptiness between the uttermost stellar systems one of those infinitesimal ripples in the creative silence of the First Cause which always occur when an exceptional stir of heightened consciousness agitates any living organism in this astronomical universe. Something passed at that moment, a wave, a motion, a vibration, too tenuous to be called magnetic, too subliminal to be called spiritual, between the soul of a particular human being who was emerging from a third-class carriage of the twelve-nineteen train from London and the divine-diabolic soul of the First Cause of all life.

—JOHN COWPER POWYS, *A Glastonbury Romance*

On February 24, 1815, the watchtower at Marseilles signaled the arrival of the three-master *Pharaon,* coming from Smyrna, Trieste and Naples.

The quay was soon covered with the usual crowd of curious onlookers, for the arrival of a ship is always a great event in Marseilles, especially when, like the *Pharaon,* it has been built, rigged and laden in the city and belongs to a local shipowner.

—ALEXANDRE DUMAS, *The Count of Monte Cristo,*
trans. Lowell Bair

At nine o'clock the auditorium of the Théâtre des Variétés was still virtually empty; a few people were waiting in the dress circle and the stalls, lost among the red velvet armchairs, in the half-light of the dimly glowing chandelier. The great red patch of the curtain was plunged in shadow, and not a sound came from the stage, the extinguished footlights, or the desks of the absent musicians.

—ÉMILE ZOLA, *Nana,* trans. George Holden

About the middle of the last century, at eight o'clock in the evening, in a large but poor apartment, a man was slumbering on a rough couch. His rusty and worn suit of black was of a piece with his uncarpeted room, the deal table of home manufacture, and its slim unsnuffed candle.

—CHARLES READE, *Peg Woffington*

On 15 May, 1796, General Bonaparte made his entry into
Milan at the head of that young army which had shortly
before crossed the Bridge of Lodi and taught the world that
after all these centuries Caesar and Alexander had a successor. The miracles of gallantry and genius of which Italy was a
witness in the space of a few months aroused a slumbering
people; only a week before the arrival of the French, the
Milanese still regarded them as a mere rabble of brigands,
accustomed invariably to flee before the troops of His Impe-
rial and Royal Majesty; so much at least was reported to
them three times weekly by a little news-sheet no bigger
than one's hand, and printed on soiled paper.

—STENDHAL, *The Charterhouse of Parma,*
trans. C. K. Scott Moncrieff

On a January evening of the early seventies, Christine Nils-
son was singing in *Faust* at the Academy of Music in New
York.

Though there was already talk of the erection, in remote
metropolitan distances "above the Forties," of a new Opera
House which should compete in costliness and splendor with
those of the great European capitals, the world of fashion was
still content to reassemble every winter in the shabby red and
gold boxes of the sociable old Academy. Conservatives cher-
ished it for being small and inconvenient, and thus keeping
out the "new people" whom New York was beginning to
dread and yet be drawn to; and the sentimental clung to it

for its historic associations, and the musical for its excellent acoustics, always so problematic a quality in halls built for the hearing of music.

—EDITH WHARTON, *The Age of Innocence*

The unusual events described in this chronicle occurred in 194— at Oran. Everyone agreed that, considering their somewhat extraordinary character, they were out of place there. For its ordinariness is what strikes one first about the town of Oran, which is merely a large French port on the Algerian coast, headquarters of the Prefect of a French Department.

—ALBERT CAMUS, *The Plague*, trans. Stuart Gilbert

It Was a Dark and Stormy Night ❧
The weather sets the mood of the story.

There was no possibility of taking a walk that day. We had been wandering, indeed, in the leafless shrubbery an hour in the morning; but since dinner (Mrs. Reed, when there was no company, dined early) the cold winter wind had brought with it clouds so sombre, and a rain so penetrating, that further outdoor exercise was now out of the question.

—CHARLOTTE BRONTË, *Jane Eyre*

To the red country and part of the gray country of Oklahoma, the last rains came gently, and they did not cut the scarred earth. The plows crossed and recrossed the rivulet marks. The last rains lifted the corn quickly and scattered weed colonies and grass along the sides of the roads so that the gray country and the dark red country began to disappear under a green cover. In the last part of May the sky grew pale and the clouds that had hung in high puffs for so long in the spring were dissipated. The sun flared down on the growing corn day after day until a line of brown spread along the edge of each green bayonet. The clouds appeared, and went away, and in a while they did not try any more. The weeds grew darker green to protect themselves, and they did not spread any more. The surface of the earth crusted, a thin hard crust, and as the sky became pale, so the earth became pale, pink in the red country and white in the gray country.

—JOHN STEINBECK, *The Grapes of Wrath*

From behind the house rises the murmuring of the river. All day long the rain has been beating against the windowpanes; a stream of water trickles down the window at the corner where it is broken. The yellowish light of the day dies down. The room is dim and dull.

—ROMAIN ROLLAND, *Jean-Christophe,* trans. Gilbert Cannan

New Start
Big Writing

I.

To the red country and part of the gray country of Oklahoma, the last rain came gently and it did not cut the scarred earth. The plows crossed and recrossed the rivulet marks. The last rains lifted the corn quickly and scattered weed colonies and grass along the sides of the roads so that the gray country and the dark red country began to disappear under a green cover. In the last part of May the sky grew pale and the clouds that had hung in high puffs for so long in the spring were dissipated. The sun flared down on the growing corn day after day until a line of brown spread along the edge of each green bayonet. The clouds appeared and went away and in a while they did not try any more. The weeds grew darker green to protect themselves and they did not spread any more. The surface of the earth crusted, a thin hard crust, and as the sky became pale so the earth became pale, pink in the red country and white in the gray country. ¶ In the water cut gullys, the earth dusted down in dry little streams. Gophers and ant lions started small avalanches. And as the sharp sun struck day after day the leaves of the young corn became less stiff and erect; they bent in a curve at first and then as the central ribs of strength grew weak, each leaf tilted downward. Then it was June and the sun shone more fiercely. The brown lines on the corn leaves widened and moved in on the central ribs. The weeds frayed and moved back toward their roots. The air was thin and the sky more pale. and every day the earth paled. ¶ In the roads where the teams moved, where the wheels milled the ground and the hooves of the horses beat the ground, the dirt crust broke and the dust formed. Every moving thing lifted the dust into the air; a walking man lifted a cloud as high as his waist, and a wagon lifted the dust as high as the fence tops, and an automobile boiled a cloud behind it. The dust was long in settling back again. ¶ When June was half gone, the big clouds moved up out of Texas and the gulf, high, heavy clouds, rain-heads. The men in the fields looked up at the clouds and snuffed at them and held wet fingers up to sense the wind. And the horses were nervous while the clouds were up. The rain heads dropped a little spattering rain and hurried on to some other country. Behind them the sky was pale again and the sun flared. In the dust there were drop craters where the rain had fallen, and there were clean splashes on the corn and that was all. ¶ A gentle wind followed the rain clouds driving them on northward, a wind that clashed the drying corn softly. A day went by and the wind increased, steady, unbroken by gusts. The dust from the roads fluffed up and spread out and fell on the weeds beside the fields, and fell into the fields a little way. Now the wind grew strong and hard, and it worked at the rain crust in the corn fields. Little by little the sky was darkened by the mixing dust, and the wind felt over the earth, loosened the dust and carried it away. The wind was stronger. The rain crust broke and the dust lifted up out of the fields and drove gray plumes into the air like sluggish smoke. The corn threshed the air and made a dry rushing sound. The finest dust did not settle back to earth now but disappeared into the darkening sky. ¶ The wind grew stronger, whisked under stones, carried up straws and old leaves, and even little clods

G
H
I
J
K
L
M
N
O
P
Q
R
S
T
U
V
W

The first page of the original manuscript of John Steinbeck's *The Grapes of Wrath*. (*The University of Virginia Library*)

There had been a heavy shower of rain, but the sun was already shining through the breaks in the clouds and throwing swiftly changing shadows on the streets, the houses, and the gardens of the city of Laurania. Everything shone wetly in the sunlight: the dust had been laid; the air was cool; the trees looked green and grateful. It was the first rain after the summer heats, and it marked the beginning of that delightful autumn climate which has made the Lauranian capital the home of the artist, the invalid, and the sybarite.

—WINSTON S. CHURCHILL, *Savrola*

The day broke gray and dull. The clouds hung heavily, and there was a rawness in the air that suggested snow. A woman servant came into a room in which a child was sleeping and drew the curtains. She glanced mechanically at the house opposite, a stucco house with a portico, and went to the child's bed.

"Wake up, Philip," she said.

She pulled down the bed-clothes, took him in her arms, and carried him downstairs. He was only half awake.

"Your mother wants you," she said.

—W. SOMERSET MAUGHAM, *Of Human Bondage*

It was a cold grey day in late November. The weather had changed overnight, when a backing wind brought a granite sky and a mizzling rain with it, and although it was now only a little after two o'clock in the afternoon the pallour of a winter evening seemed to have closed upon the hills, cloaking them in mist. It would be dark by four.

—DAPHNE DU MAURIER, *Jamaica Inn*

Thirty years ago, Marseilles lay burning in the sun, one day.

A blazing sun upon a fierce August day was no greater rarity in southern France then, than at any other time, before or since. Everything in Marseilles, and about Marseilles, had stared at the fervid sky, and been stared at in return, until a staring habit had become universal there. Strangers were stared out of countenance by staring white houses, staring white walls, staring white streets, staring tracts of arid road, staring hills from which verdure was burnt away. The only things to be seen not fixedly staring and glaring were the vines drooping under their load of grapes. These did occasionally wink a little, as the hot air barely moved their faint leaves.

—CHARLES DICKENS, *Little Dorrit*

All day the heat had been barely supportable but at evening a breeze arose in the West, blowing from the heart of the setting sun and from the ocean, which lay unseen, unheard behind the scrubby foothills. It shook the rusty fringes of palm-leaf and swelled the dry sounds of summer, the frog-voices, the grating cicadas, and the ever present pulse of music from the neighbouring native huts.

—EVELYN WAUGH, *The Loved One*

A Saturday afternoon in November was approaching the time of twilight, and the vast tract of unenclosed wild known as Egdon Heath embrowned itself moment by moment. Overhead the hollow stretch of whitish cloud shutting out the sky was as a tent which had the whole heath for its floor.

—THOMAS HARDY, *The Return of the Native*

To-day a rare sun of spring. And horse carts clanging to the quays down Tara Street and the shoeless white-faced kids screaming.

—J. P. DONLEAVY, *The Ginger Man*

It was a fine, sunny, showery day in April.

The big studio window was open at the top, and let in a pleasant breeze from the north-west. Things were beginning to look shipshape at last.

—GEORGE DU MAURIER, *Trilby*

Early in the morning between winter and spring, when the grass is frosty, when there is no scent and no sound but a heavy white stillness, and yet you know the blackbird may speak at any moment, a sharp sweet waterfall of sound fall down, and the earth wake—on such a morning the milkman whistles 'Auprès de ma blonde' as he drives down the little alley behind the houses on the Boulevard Léopold.

—MAY SARTON, *The Single Hound*

At five o'clock in the afternoon, which was late in March, the stainless blue of the sky over Rome had begun to pale and the blue transparency of the narrow streets had gathered a faint opacity of vapor. Domes of ancient churches, swelling above the angular roofs like the breasts of recumbent giant women, still bathed in gold light, and so did the very height of that immense cascade of stone stairs that descended from the Trinita di Monte to the Piazza di Spagna.

—TENNESSEE WILLIAMS, *The Roman Spring of Mrs. Stone*

A low pale lemon grey sun hung over the winter moor. It swam, haloed, in the grey mist. The road climbed gently into obscurity. Dimly on either side appeared straw-grey tufts of long grasses, pale reeds, patches of dwindling, lingering snow. Grey shades, yellow shades, a soft damp white light. Alix Bowen gazed ahead, exalted. She was on her way to see her murderer. Her heart sang, in the cold landscape, as she drove towards the flat summit of the moor.

—MARGARET DRABBLE, *A Natural Curiosity*

It was a bright cold day in April, and the clocks were striking thirteen. Winston Smith, his chin nuzzled into his breast in an effort to escape the vile wind, slipped quickly through the glass doors of Victory Mansions, though not quickly enough to prevent a swirl of gritty dust from entering along with him.

—GEORGE ORWELL, *1984*

The cold passed reluctantly from the earth, and the retiring fogs revealed an army stretched out on the hills, resting. As the landscape changed from brown to green, the army awakened, and began to tremble with eagerness at the noise of rumors. It cast its eyes upon the roads, which were growing from long troughs of liquid mud to proper thoroughfares. A river, amber-tinted in the shadow of its banks, purled at the army's feet; and at night, when the stream had become of a sorrowful blackness, one could see across it the red, eyelike gleam of hostile camp-fires set in the low brows of distant hills.

—STEPHEN CRANE, *The Red Badge of Courage*

That morning's ice, no more than a brittle film, had cracked and was now floating in segments. These tapped together or, parting, left channels of dark water, down which swans in slow indignation swam. The island stood in frozen woody brown dusk: it was now between three and four in the afternoon. A sort of breath from the clay, from the city outside the park, condensing, made the air unclear; through this, the trees round the lake soared frigidly up. Bronze cold of January bound the sky and the landscape; the sky was shut to the sun—but the swans, the rims of the ice, the pallid withdrawn Regency terraces had an unnatural burnish, as though cold were light. There is something momentous about the height of winter. Steps rang on the bridges, and along the black walks. This weather had set in; it would freeze harder tonight.

—ELIZABETH BOWEN, *The Death of the Heart*

The sun had not yet risen. The sea was indistinguishable from the sky, except that the sea was slightly creased as if a cloth had wrinkles in it. Gradually as the sky whitened a dark line lay on the horizon dividing the sea from the sky and the grey cloth became barred with thick strokes moving, one after another, beneath the surface, following each other, pursuing each other, perpetually.

—VIRGINIA WOOLF, *The Waves*

The sea is high again today, with a thrilling flush of wind. In the midst of winter you can feel the inventions of Spring. A sky of hot nude pearl until midday, crickets in sheltered places, and now the wind unpacking the great planes, ransacking the great planes. . . .

—LAWRENCE DURRELL, *Justine*

The sea which lies before me as I write glows rather than sparkles in the bland May sunshine. With the tide turning, it leans quietly against the land, almost unflecked by ripples or by foam. Near to the horizon it is a luxurious purple, spotted with regular lines of emerald green. At the horizon it is indigo. Near to the shore, where my view is framed by rising heaps of humpy yellow rock, there is a band of lighter green, icy and pure, less radiant, opaque however, not transparent.

—IRIS MURDOCH, *The Sea, The Sea*

The Sea lost nothing of the swallowing identity of its great
outer mass of waters in the emphatic, individual character of
each particular wave. Each wave, as it rolled in upon the
high-pebbled beach, was an epitome of the whole body of
the sea, and carried with it all the vast mysterious quality of
the earth's ancient antagonist.

—JOHN COWPER POWYS, *Weymouth Sands*

Only the steady creaking of a flight of swans disturbed the
silence, labouring low overhead with outstretched necks
toward the sea.

It was a warm, wet, windless afternoon with a soft feathery
feeling in the air: rain, yet so fine it could scarcely fall but rather
floated. It clung to everything it touched; the rushes in the deep
choked ditches of the sea-marsh were bowed down with it, the
small black cattle looked cobwebbed with it, their horns were
jewelled with it. Curiously stumpy too these cattle looked, the
whole herd sunk nearly to the knees in a soft patch.

—RICHARD HUGHES, *The Fox in the Attic*

I was walking by the Thames. Half-past morning on an
autumn day. Sun in a mist. Like an orange in a fried fish
shop. All bright below. Low tide, dusty water and a crooked
bar of straw, chicken boxes, dirt and oil from mud to mud.
Like a viper swimming in skim milk. The old serpent, symbol of nature and love.

—JOYCE CARY, *The Horse's Mouth*

7 ❧ THE PLOT'S THE THING

A match strikes, a gun reports, reveille sounds, something is happening.

The decision to begin a story with action is to a large extent a defensive one: a reader not caught by the first page is probably a lost reader. There are exceptions of course, novels where the power of the author's reputation or the book's critical acclaim will induce him to hold on, but for the most part, today's reader has neither time nor patience for long, leisured Jamesian beginnings.

The alternative is to start with Something Happening, preferably something unusual or shocking. As we open Larry McMurtry's *Lonesome Dove,* the action, if rather repugnant, is nevertheless fascinating: "When Augustus came out on the porch the blue pigs were eating a rattlesnake—not a very big one." The sentence pretty well guarantees the reader will read on—at least to the next sentence.

If the action is more than an isolated arresting episode, but is intrinsic to the plot, all the better. So we find novels that begin with crowd scenes, novels that begin with deaths, novels that begin with journeys; the plot is already in motion. (Boris Pasternak managed to combine both a death *and* a journey in *Doctor Zhivago*, with the funeral procession of Zhivago's wife.) These active openings carry their own excitement with them. Before we finish the first sentence, we are already asking the question every novelist must keep in the mind of his reader until the final page: "What is going to happen next?"

Mystery is at the heart of any successful plot, and in a novel as in life, nothing intrigues our curiosity as much as the arrival of an unidentified stranger. Often the catalyst to the story, the stranger appeals to our human voyeuristic tendencies, and we are prepared to hear more when novelists as diverse as Dostoyevsky, Sinclair Lewis, John Fowles, and Georgette Heyer begin with some variation of "A girl was seen walking ..." Sometimes "three young men are seen sitting at a cafe," and some have even been "sighted on a train," but the result is the same: we want to know what they are doing and are willing to stoop to eavesdropping to find out.

Action! ✍

We arrive on the scene just in time; the story's begun.

When Augustus came out on the porch the blue pigs were eating a rattlesnake—not a very big one. It had probably just

been crawling around looking for shade when it ran into the
pigs. They were having a fine tug-of-war with it, and its rattling days were over. The sow had it by the neck, and the
shoat had the tail.

—LARRY MCMURTRY, *Lonesome Dove*

Jinn and Phyllis were spending a wonderful holiday, in space,
as far away as possible from the inhabited stars.
   In those days interplanetary voyages were an everyday
occurrence, and interstellar travel not uncommon.

—PIERRE BOULLE, *Planet of the Apes,* trans. Xan Fielding

The schoolmaster was leaving the village, and everybody
seemed sorry. The miller at Cresscombe lent him the
small white tilted cart and horse to carry his goods to the
city of his destination, about twenty miles off, such a vehicle
proving of quite sufficient size for the departing teacher's
effects.

—THOMAS HARDY, *Jude the Obscure*

Someone must have been telling lies about Joseph K., for
without having done anything wrong he was arrested one
fine morning. His landlady's cook, who always brought him
his breakfast at eight o'clock, failed to appear on this occa-
sion. That had never happened before.

—FRANZ KAFKA, *The Trial*

The cell door slammed behind Rubashov.

He remained leaning against the door for a few seconds, and lit a cigarette. On the bed to his right lay two fairly clean blankets, and the straw mattress looked newly filled. The wash-basin to his left had no plug, but the tap functioned. The can next to it had been freshly disinfected, it did not smell.

—ARTHUR KOESTLER, *Darkness at Noon*,
trans. Daphne Hardy

Through the fence, between the curling flower spaces, I could see them hitting. They were coming toward where the flag was and I went along the fence. Luster was hunting in the grass by the flower tree. They took the flag out, and they were hitting. Then they put the flag back and they went to the table, and he hit and the other hit. Then they went on, and I went along the fence. Luster came away from the flower tree and we went along the fence and they stopped and we stopped and I looked through the fence while Luster was hunting in the grass.

"Here, caddie."

—WILLIAM FAULKNER, *The Sound and the Fury*

So great and deep a cave, of course, had to be dark. But it was even darker than François had expected when he crawled through the narrow entrance. Then he could tell from the feel of the sand underneath his hands that he was inside it in depth.

—LAURENS VAN DER POST, *A Far-Off Place*

The match scratched noisily across the rusted metal of the corrugated iron shed, fizzled, then burst into a sputtering pool of light, the harsh sound and sudden brilliance alike strangely alien in the stillness of the desert night. Mechanically, Mallory's eyes followed the cupped sweep of the flaring match to the cigarette jutting out beneath the commodore's clipped moustache, saw the light stop inches away from the face, saw too the sudden stillness of that face, the unfocused vacancy of the eyes of a man lost in listening. Then the match was gone, ground into the sand of the airfield perimeter.

—ALISTAIR MACLEAN, *The Guns of Navarone*

Several yards of undermined sand and clay broke loose up near the top, and the land slid down to the floor of the crater. Ty Ty Walden was so angry about the landslide that he just stood there with the pick in his hands, knee-deep in the reddish earth, and swore about everything he could think of.

—ERSKINE CALDWELL, *God's Little Acre*

Reveille was sounded, as always, at 5 A.M..—a hammer pounding on a rail outside camp HQ. The ringing noise came faintly on and off through the windowpanes covered with ice more than an inch thick, and died away fast. It was cold and the warder didn't feel like going on banging.

—ALEXANDER SOLZHENITSYN, *One Day in the Life of Ivan Denisovich,* trans. Max Hayward and Ronald Hingley

The bench on which Dobbs was sitting was not so good. One of the slats was broken; the one next to it was bent so that to have to sit on it was a sort of punishment. If Dobbs deserved punishment, or if this punishment was being inflicted upon him unjustly, as most punishments are, such a thought did not enter his head at this moment.

—B. TRAVEN, *The Treasure of the Sierra Madre*

The boy with fair hair lowered himself down the last few feet of rock and began to pick his way toward the lagoon. Though he had taken off his school sweater and trailed it now from one hand, his grey shirt stuck to him and his hair was plastered to his forehead. All round him the long scar smashed into the jungle was a bath of heat. He was clambering heavily among the creepers and broken trunks when a bird, a vision of red and yellow, flashed upwards with a witch-like cry; and this cry was echoed by another.

"Hi!" it said. "Wait a minute!"

—WILLIAM GOLDING, *Lord of the Flies*

As the Milvains sat down to breakfast the clock of Wattleborough parish church struck eight; it was two miles away, but the strokes were borne very distinctly on the west wind this autumn morning. Jasper, listening before he cracked an egg, remarked with cheerfulness:

"There's a man being hanged in London at this moment."

—GEORGE GISSING, *New Grub Street*

Strether's first question, when he reached the hotel, was about his friend; yet on learning that Waymarsh was apparently not to arrive till evening he was not wholly disconcerted. A telegram from him bespeaking a room "only if not noisy," reply paid, was produced for the enquirer at the office, so that the understanding they should meet at Chester rather than at Liverpool remained to that extent sound.

—HENRY JAMES, *The Ambassadors*

They were to have met in the garden of the *Chapelle Expiatoire* at five o'clock in the afternoon, but Julio Desnoyers with the impatience of a lover who hopes to advance the moment of meeting by presenting himself before the appointed time, arrived an half hour earlier. The change of the seasons was at this time greatly confused in his mind, and evidently demanded some readjustment.

—VICENTE BLASCO IBAÑEZ, *The Four Horsemen of the Apocalypse*

Thirteen's a Crowd ∾
We join a group to see what's going on.

The men at work at the corner of the street had made a kind of camp for themselves, where, marked out by tripods hung with red hurricane-lamps, an abyss in the road led down to a network of subterranean drain-pipes. Gathered round the bucket of coke that burned in front of the shelter, several fig-

ures were swinging arms against bodies and rubbing hands together with large, pantomimic gestures: like comedians giving formal expression to the concept of extreme cold.
—ANTHONY POWELL, *A Dance to the Music of Time*

Boys are playing basketball around a telephone pole with a backboard bolted to it. Legs, shouts. The scrape and snap of Keds on loose alley pebbles seems to catapult their voices high into the moist March air blue above the wires. Rabbit Angstrom, coming up the alley in a business suit, stops and watches, though he's twenty-six and six three.
—JOHN UPDIKE, *Rabbit, Run*

The yard was all silent and empty under the burning afternoon heat, which had made its asphalt springy like turf, when suddenly the children threw themselves out of the great doors at either end of the Sunday-school—boys from the right, girls from the left—in two howling, impetuous streams, that widened, eddied, intermingled and formed backwaters until the whole quadrangle was full of clamour and movement.
—ARNOLD BENNETT, *Anna of the Five Towns*

It was the evening on which MM. Debienne and Poligny, the managers of the Opera, were giving a last gala performance to mark their retirement. Suddenly the dressing-room

of La Sorelli, one of the principal dancers, was invaded by
half-a-dozen young ladies of the ballet, who had come up
from the stage after "dancing" *Polyeucte.* They rushed in amid
great confusion, some giving vent to forced and unnatural
laughter, others to cries of terror. Sorelli, who wished to be
alone for a moment to "run through" the speech which she
was to make to the resigning managers, looked around angrily at the mad and tumultuous crowd. It was little Jammes—
the girl with the tip-tilted nose, the forget-me-not eyes, the
rose-red cheeks and the lily-white neck and shoulders—who
gave the explanation in a trembling voice:

"It's the ghost!" And she locked the door.

—GASTON LEROUX, *The Phantom of the Opera*

A surging, seething, murmuring crowd of beings that are
human only in name, for to the eye and ear they seem
naught but savage creatures, animated by vile passions and by
the lust of vengeance and of hate. The hour, some little time
before sunset, and the place, the West Barricade, at the very
spot where, a decade later, a proud tyrant raised an undying
monument to the nation's glory and his own vanity.

During the greater part of the day the guillotine had been
kept busy at its ghastly work: all that France had boasted of
in the past centuries, of ancient names, and blue blood, had
paid toll to her desire for liberty and for fraternity. The car-
nage had only ceased at this late hour of the day because
there were other more interesting sights for the people to

witness, a little while before the final closing of the barricades for the night.

—BARONESS ORCZY, *The Scarlet Pimpernel*

The rowdy gang of singers who sat at the scattered tables saw Arthur walk unsteadily to the head of the stairs, and though they must all have known that he was dead drunk, and seen the danger he would soon be in, no one attempted to talk to him and lead him back to his seat. With eleven pints of beer and seven small gins playing hide-and-seek inside his stomach, he fell from the top-most stair to the bottom.

—ALAN SILLITOE, *Saturday Night and Sunday Morning*

The boys, as they talked to the girls from Marcia Blaine School, stood on the far side of their bicycles holding the handlebars, which established a protective fence of bicycle between the sexes, and the impression that at any moment the boys were likely to be away.

The girls could not take off their panama hats because this was not far from the school gates and hatlessness was an offence.

—MURIEL SPARK, *The Prime of Miss Jean Brodie*

From the small crossed window of his room above the stable in the brickyard, Yakov Bok saw people in their long overcoats running somewhere early that morning, everybody in the same direction. Vey iz mir, he thought uneasily, something bad has happened.

—BERNARD MALAMUD, *The Fixer*

A throng of bearded men, in sad-colored garments, and gray, steeple-crowned hats, intermixed with women, some wearing hoods, and others bareheaded, was assembled in front of a wooden edifice, the door of which was heavily timbered with oak, and studded with iron spikes.

The founders of a new colony, whatever Utopia of human virtue and happiness they might originally project, have invariably recognized it among their earliest practical necessities to allot a portion of the virgin soil as a cemetery, and another portion as the site of a prison.

—NATHANIEL HAWTHORNE, *The Scarlet Letter*

A Girl Was Seen Walking ⌘
The author begins with the arrival of a stranger.

On a hill by the Mississippi where Chippewas camped two generations ago, a girl stood in relief against the cornflower blue of Northern sky. She saw no Indians now; she saw flour-mills and the blinking windows of skyscrapers in Minneapolis and St. Paul. Nor was she thinking of squaws and portages, and the Yankee fur-traders whose shadows were all about her. She was meditating upon walnut fudge, the plays of Brieux, the reasons why heels run over, and the fact that the chemistry instructor had stared at the new coiffure which concealed her ears.

—SINCLAIR LEWIS, *Main Street*

A girl and an older woman were walking along a metaled pathway. To their left, beyond a strip of grass, was the front of a large high building in grey stone. Reaching its corner, at which there was a pointed turret, brought them a view of a square of grass on which stood a tower-like structure supported by stone pillars. The afternoon sun was shining brightly and the space under the main part of the tower was in deep shadow.

The girl halted. "What's happening?" she asked.

—KINGSLEY AMIS, *The Anti-Death League*

On an exceptionally hot evening early in July a young man came out of the garret in which he lodged in S. Place and walked slowly, as though in hesitation, towards K. bridge. He had successfully avoided meeting his landlady on the staircase. His garret was under the roof of a high, five-storied house and was more like a cupboard than a room. The landlady who provided him with garret, dinners, and attendance, lived on the floor below, and every time he went out he was obliged to pass her kitchen, the door of which invariably stood open. And each time he passed, the young man had a sick, frightened feeling, which made him scowl and feel ashamed. He was hopelessly in debt to his landlady, and was afraid of meeting her.

—FYODOR DOSTOYEVSKY, *Crime and Punishment,*
trans. Constance Garnett

A gentleman was strolling down a side street in Paris, on his way back from the house of one Madame de Verchoureux. He walked mincingly, for the red heels of his shoes were very high. A long purple cloak, rose-lined, hung from his shoulders and was allowed to fall carelessly back from his dress, revealing a full-skirted coat of purple satin, heavily laced with gold; a waistcoat of flowered silk; faultless small clothes; and a lavish sprinkling of jewels on his cravat and breast.

—GEORGETTE HEYER, *These Old Shades*

Late in the afternoon of a chilly day in February, two gentlemen were sitting alone over their wine, in a well-furnished dining parlor, in the town of P_____, in Kentucky. There were no servants present, and the gentlemen, with chairs closely approaching, seemed to be discussing some subject with great earnestness.

—HARRIET BEECHER STOWE, *Uncle Tom's Cabin*

At the ten-second warning to the evening's first preliminary, a newspaperman on the apron of the ring stood up to get his slicker off. He had the right arm out and was pulling at the left while watching a Mexican featherweight in the corner above his head. At the bell he left the sleeve dangling: to see a Pole with an army haircut come out of the opposite corner straight into the Mexican's left hand. The army haircut went back on his heels, stopped dead, and glanced unbelievingly at the Mex; then kept coming in.

—NELSON ALGREN, *Never Come Morning*

The evening before my departure for Blithedale, I was returning to my bachelor-apartments, after attending the wonderful exhibition of the Veiled Lady, when an elderly-man of rather shabby appearance met me in an obscure part of the street.

"Mr. Coverdale," said he, softly, "can I speak with you a moment?"

—NATHANIEL HAWTHORNE, *The Blithedale Romance*

On an evening in the latter part of May a middle-aged man was walking homeward from Shaston to the village of Marlott, in the adjoining vale of Blakemore or Blackmoor. The pair of legs that carried him were rickety, and there was a bias in his gait which inclined him somewhat to the left of a straight line. He occasionally gave a smart nod, as if in confirmation of some opinion, though he was not thinking of anything in particular. An empty egg-basket was slung upon his arm, the nap of his hat was ruffled, a patch being quite worn away at its brim where his thumb came in taking it off.

Presently he was met by an elderly parson astride on a gray mare, who, as he rode, hummed a wandering tune.

'Good night t'ee,' said the man with the basket.

'Good night, Sir John,' said the parson.

—THOMAS HARDY, *Tess of the d'Urbervilles*

An easterly is the most disagreeable wind in Lyme Bay—Lyme Bay being that largest bite from the underside of England's outstretched southwestern leg—and a person of curiosity could at once have deduced several strong probabilities about the pair who began to walk down the quay at Lyme Regis, the small but ancient eponym of the inbite, one incisively sharp and blustery morning in the late March of 1867.

The Cobb has invited what familiarity breeds for at least seven hundred years, and the real Lymers will never see much more to it than a long claw of old gray wall that flexes itself against the sea.

—JOHN FOWLES, *The French Lieutenant's Woman*

I was leaning against the bar in a speakeasy on Fifty-second Street, waiting for Nora to finish her Christmas shopping, when a girl got up from the table where she had been sitting with three other people and came over to me. She was small and blonde, and whether you looked at her face or at her body in powder-blue sports clothes, the result was satisfactory. "Aren't you Nick Charles?" she asked.

—DASHIELL HAMMETT, *The Thin Man*

On the Road ∾
The story is already in motion—on a ship, in a carriage, in the air.

On they went, singing "Rest Eternal," and whenever they stopped, their feet, the horses, and the gusts of wind seemed to carry on their singing.

Passers-by made way for the procession, counted the wreaths, and crossed themselves. Some joined in out of curiosity and asked: "Who is being buried?"—"Zhivago," they were told.—"Oh, I see. That's what it is."—"It isn't him. It's his wife."—"Well, it comes to the same thing. May her soul rest in peace. It's a fine funeral."

—BORIS PASTERNAK, *Doctor Zhivago*,
trans. Max Hayward and Manya Harari

Mr. Baker, chief mate of the ship *Narcissus,* stepped in one stride out of his lighted cabin into the darkness of the quarter-deck. Above his head on the break of the poop, the night watchman rang a double stroke. It was nine o'clock. Mr. Baker, speaking up to the man above him, asked: "Are all the hands aboard, Knowles?"

—JOSEPH CONRAD, *The Nigger of the "Narcissus"*

The two young men—they were of the English public official class—sat in the perfectly appointed railway carriage. The leather straps to the windows were of virgin newness; the mirrors beneath the new luggage racks immaculate as if they had reflected very little; the bulging upholstery in its luxuriant, regulated curves was scarlet and yellow in an intricate, minute dragon pattern, the design of a geometrician in Cologne. The compartment smelt faintly, hygienically of admirable varnish; the train ran as smoothly—Tietjens remembered thinking—as British gilt-edged securities.

—FORD MADOX FORD, *Parade's End*

On Tuesday the freighter steamed through the Straits of Gibraltar and for five days plowed eastward through the Mediterranean, past islands and peninsulas rich in history, so that on Saturday night the steward advised Dr. Cullinane, "If you wish an early sight of the Holy Land you must be up at dawn." The steward was Italian and was reluctant to use the name Israel. For him, good Catholic that he was, it would always be the Holy Land.

—JAMES A. MICHENER, *The Source*

The slow train puffed away into the unadventurous country; and the bees buzzing round the wine-dark dahlias along the platform were once again audible. The last farewell that Guy Hazlewood flung over his shoulder to a parting friend was more casual than it would have been, had he not at the same moment been turning to ask the solitary porter how many cases of books awaited his disposition.

—COMPTON MACKENZIE, *Guy and Pauline*

There were 117 psychoanalysts on the Pan Am flight to Vienna and I'd been treated by at least six of them. And married a seventh. God knows it was a tribute either to the shrinks' ineptitude or my own glorious unanalyzability that I was now, if anything, more scared of flying than when I began my analytic adventures some thirteen years earlier.

—ERICA JONG, *Fear of Flying*

Some notable sight was drawing the passengers, both men and women, to the window; and therefore I rose and crossed the car to see what it was. I saw near the track an enclosure, and round it some laughing men, and inside it some whirling dust, and amid the dust some horses, plunging, huddling, and dodging. They were cow ponies in a corral, and one of them would not be caught, no matter who threw the rope.

—OWEN WISTER, *The Virginian*

This March day the vast and brassy sky, always spangled with the silver glint of airplanes, roared and glittered with celestial traffic. Gigantic though they loomed against the white-hot heavens there was nothing martial about these winged mammoths. They were merely private vehicles bearing nice little alligator jewel cases and fabulous gowns and overbred furs.

—EDNA FERBER, *Giant*

The airplane pip-plopped down the runway to a halt before the big sign: WELCOME TO CYPRUS. Mark Parker looked out of the window and in the distance he could see the jagged wonder of the Peak of Five Fingers of the northern coastal range. In an hour or so he would be driving through the pass to Kyrenia. He stepped into the aisle, straightened out his necktie, rolled down his sleeves, and slipped into his jacket. "Welcome to Cyprus, welcome to Cyprus …" It ran through his head. It was from *Othello,* he thought, but the full quotation slipped his mind.

—LEON URIS, *Exodus*

A rather pretty little chaise on springs, such as bachelors, half-pay officers, staff captains, landowners with about a hundred serfs—in short, all such as are spoken of as "gentlemen of the middling sort"—drive about in, rolled in at the gates of the hotel of the provincial town of N. In the chaise sat a gentleman, not handsome but not bad-looking, not too stout and not too thin; it could not be said that he was old, neither could he be described as extremely young. His arrival in the town created no sensation whatever and was not accompanied by anything remarkable.

—NIKOLAI GOGOL, *Dead Souls,* trans. Constance Garnett

The driver of the wagon swaying through forest and swamp of the Ohio wilderness was a ragged girl of fourteen. Her mother they had buried near the Monongahela—the girl herself had heaped with torn sods the grave beside the river of the beautiful name. Her father lay shrinking with fever on the floor of the wagon-box, and about him played her brothers and sisters, dirty brats, tattered brats, hilarious brats.

—SINCLAIR LEWIS, *Arrowsmith*

Through the late afternoon they flew southeast, going home to Ocanara at about two hundred miles an hour. Inside the spic and span fuselage—the plane was a new twin-engine advanced trainer of the type designated AT-7—this speed was not noticeable. Though the engines steadily and powerfully vibrated and time was passing, the shining plane seemed stationary, swaying gently and slightly oscillating, a little higher than the stationary, dull-crimson sphere of the low sun.

—JAMES GOULD COZZENS, *Guard of Honor*

The boat's whistle was a lament, piercing the twilight that lay upon the town. Standing upon the deck, Captain João Magalhães surveyed the jumble of old-fashioned houses, the church spires, the dark roof-tops, the streets paved with enormous cobblestones. His gaze took in the roofs of varying shape, but he had no more than a glimpse of a bit of street where no one passed.

—JORGE AMADO, *The Violent Land,* trans. Samuel Putnam

The Sergeant takes a look at Sister Patrocinio and the botfly is still there. The launch is pitching on the muddy waters, between two walls of trees that give off a burning, sticky mist. Huddled under the canopy, stripped to the waist, the soldiers are asleep, with the greenish, yellowish noonday sun above: Shorty's head is lying on Fats's stomach, Blondy is breathing in short bursts, Blacky has his mouth open and is grunting. A thin shadow of gnats is escorting the launch, and butterflies, wasps, horseflies take shape among the bodies.

—MARIO VARGAS LLOSA, *The Green House,*
trans. Gregory Rabassa

It was the second day of their journey to their first home. Lana, in the cart, looked back to see how her husband was making out with the cow. He had bought it from the Domine for a wedding present to her. He had hesitated a long while between the cow and the clock; and she had been disappointed when he finally decided on the cow, even though it cost three dollars more; but now she admitted that it would be a fine thing to have a cow to milk. As he said, it would give her companionship when he was working in the woods.

—WALTER D. EDMONDS, *Drums Along the Mohawk*

Death as a Beginning ∼
The author uses death as the circumstance that sets the story in motion.

When her father died, Laura Willowes went to live in London with her elder brother and his family.

"Of course," said Caroline, "you will come to us."

"But it will upset all your plans. It will give you so much trouble. Are you sure you really want me?"

"Oh *dear*, yes."

—SYLVIA TOWNSEND WARNER, *Lolly Willowes*

I wake ... the touch of that cold object against my penis awakens me. I did not know that at times one can urinate without knowing it. I keep my eyes closed. The nearest voices cannot be heard: if I opened my eyes, would I hear them? But my eyelids are heavy, they are lead, and there are brass coins on my tongue and iron hammers in my ears and something, something, something like tarnished silver in my breathing; metal, everything is metal; or again, mineral.

—CARLOS FUENTES, *The Death of Artemio Cruz*, trans. Sam Hileman

But old Mrs. Goodman did die at last.

Theodora went into the room where the coffin lay. She moved one hairbrush three inches to the left, and smoothed the antimacassar on a little Empire prie-dieu that her mother had brought from Europe. She did all this with some surprise, as if divorced from her own hands, as if they were related to the objects beneath them only in the way that two flies, blowing and blundering in space, are related to a china and mahogany world. It was all very surprising, the accomplished as opposed to the contemplated fact. It had altered the silence of the house. It had altered the room. This was

GREAT BEGINNINGS ❧ 123

no longer the bedroom of her mother. It was a waiting room, which housed the shiny box that contained a wax-work.

—PATRICK WHITE, *The Aunt's Story*

Long after the hours when tradesmen are in the habit of commencing business, the shutters of a certain shop in the town of Lymport-on-the-Sea remained significantly closed, and it became known that death had taken Mr. Melchisedec Harrington, and struck one off the list of living tailors. The demise of a respectable member of this class does not ordinarily create a profound sensation. He dies, and his equals debate who is to be his successor: while the rest of them who have come in contact with him, very probably hear nothing of his great launch and final adieu till the winding up of cash-accounts; on which occasions we may augur that he is not often blessed by one or other of the two great parties who subdivide this universe. In the case of Mr. Melchisedec it was otherwise. This had been a grand man, despite his calling, and in the teeth of opprobrious epithets against his craft.

—GEORGE MEREDITH, *Evan Harrington*

It was inevitable: the scent of bitter almonds always reminded him of the fate of unrequited love. Dr. Juvenal Urbino noticed it as soon as he entered the still darkened house where he had hurried on an urgent call to attend a case that for him had lost all urgency many years before. The Antillean refugee Jeremiah de Saint-Amour, disabled war veteran, photographer of children, and his most sympathetic opponent in chess, had escaped the torments of memory with the aromatic fumes of gold cyanide.

—GABRIEL GARCÍA MÁRQUEZ, *Love in the Time of Cholera*, trans. Edith Grossman

Mrs. Ferrars died on the night of the 16th–17th September—a Thursday. I was sent for at eight o'clock on the morning of Friday the 17th. There was nothing to be done. She had been dead some hours.

—AGATHA CHRISTIE, *The Murder of Roger Ackroyd*

Francis Marion Tarwater's uncle had been dead for only half a day when the boy got too drunk to finish digging his grave and a Negro named Buford Munson, who had come to get a jug filled, had to finish it and drag the body from the breakfast table where it was still sitting and bury it in a decent and Christian way, with the sign of its Saviour at the head of the grave and enough dirt on top to keep the dogs from digging it up. Buford had come along about noon and when he left at sundown, the boy, Tarwater, had never returned from the still.

—FLANNERY O'CONNOR, *The Violent Bear It Away*

Fedora was dead, and who could talk of anything else? Including the entire staff of *Good Morning USA,* whose producer wanted a twenty-minute air-time recap of the actress's illustrious career, with "fresh angles" and "a new slant." Marion Walker wondered what there was to say about Fedora that hadn't already been said.

—THOMAS TRYON, *Crowned Heads*

As usual, old man Falls had brought John Sartoris into the room with him, had walked the three miles in from the county Poor Farm, fetching, like an odor, like the clean dusty smell of his faded overalls, the spirit of the dead man into that room where the dead man's son sat and where the two of them, pauper and banker, would sit for a half an hour in the company of him who had passed beyond death and then returned.

—WILLIAM FAULKNER, *Sartoris*

8 ⚘ THE QUOTATION

novel that begins with dialogue presents us with much the same experience as entering a room in the middle of a conversation. Our perception of what is going on depends on the fragment of conversation that we hear, and from it and the responses that follow, we begin to piece together a story. Once again we are thrust into the middle of the action and of a plot that is already underway. Naturally, the extent of our interest will depend on the quality of what we overhear. Hopefully, the reader will ask, as eight-year old Antonie does in the first line of Thomas Mann's *Buddenbrooks,* "And—and—what comes next?" "What do you think she'd do if she caught us?" Kipling's young Maisie asks Dick Heldar in *The Light That Failed,* and we want to know what terrible thing the children have done. Through the opening dialogue, we receive our first impression of the speaker, and, if that person is the main character, an indication of his or her voice, intellect, social class, and nature. As long as the opening quotation interests us, it doesn't have to be overly clever, although some authors strive for the unusual; it is difficult to ignore an opening like Rose Macaulay's, "Take my camel, dear," in *The Towers of Trebizond.*

Some authors, among them Kingsley Amis, have relied quite extensively on dialogue openings. With great success, because the quotation, which takes advantage of our instinct to eavesdrop, is such a natural way to begin.

"What's That?" ∾
The action has already begun, and we are there.

"Well, Prince, Genoa and Lucca are now no more than private estates of the Bonaparte family. No, I warn you, that if you do not tell me we are at war, if you again allow yourself to palliate all the infamies and atrocities of this Antichrist (upon my word, I believe he is), I don't know you in future, you are no longer my friend, no longer my faithful slave, as you say. There, how do you do, how do you do? I see I'm scaring you, sit down and talk to me."

—COUNT LEO TOLSTOY, *War and Peace,*
trans. Constance Garnett

"They made a silly mistake, though," the Professor of History said, and his smile, as Dixon watched, gradually sank beneath the surface of his features at the memory. "After the interval we did a little piece by Dowland," he went on; "for recorder and keyboard, you know. I played the recorder, of course, and young Johns ..." He paused, and his trunk grew rigid as he walked; it was as if some entirely different man, some imposter who couldn't copy his voice, had momentarily taken his place; then he went on again: "... young Johns played the piano. . . ."

—KINGSLEY AMIS, *Lucky Jim*

"Christmas won't be Christmas without any presents," grumbled Jo, lying on the rug.

"It's so dreadful to be poor!" sighed Meg, looking down at her old dress.

"I don't think it's fair for some girls to have plenty of pretty things and other girls nothing at all," added little Amy, with an injured sniff.

"We've got father and mother and each other," said Beth contentedly, from her corner.

—LOUISA MAY ALCOTT, *Little Women*

"What do you think she'd do if she caught us? We oughtn't to have it, you know," said Maisie.

"Beat me, and lock you up in your bedroom," Dick answered, without hesitation. "Have you got the cartridges?"

—RUDYARD KIPLING, *The Light that Failed*

Hi, teach!

Looka *her!* She's a teacher?

Who she?

Is this 304? Are you Mr. Barringer?

No. I'm Miss Barrett.

I'm supposed to have Mr. Barringer.

I'm Miss Barrett.

You the teacher? You so young.

Hey, she's cute! Hey, teach, can I be in your class?

Please don't block the doorway. Please come in.

Good afternoon, Miss Barnet.

Miss Barrett. My name is on the blackboard. Good morning.

—BEL KAUFMAN, *Up the Down Staircase*

"And—and—what comes next?"

"Oh, yes, yes, what the dickens does come next? *C'est la question, ma très chère demoiselle!*"

Frau Consul Buddenbrook shot a glance at her husband and came to the rescue of her little daughter.

—THOMAS MANN, *Buddenbrooks,* trans. H. T. Lowe-Porter

"Kaspar! Makan!"

The well-known shrill voice startled Almayer from his dream of splendid future into the unpleasant realities of the present hour. An unpleasant voice too. He had heard it for many years, and with every year he liked it less. No matter; there would be an end to all this soon.

—JOSEPH CONRAD, *Almayer's Folly*

"Yes, of course, if it's fine tomorrow," said Mrs. Ramsay. "But you'll have to be up with the lark," she added.

To her son these words conveyed an extraordinary joy, as if it were settled, the expedition were bound to take place, and the wonder to which he had looked forward, for years and years it seemed, was, after a night's darkness and a day's sail, within touch.

—VIRGINIA WOOLF, *To the Lighthouse*

"Tom!"

No answer.

"Tom!"

No answer.

"What's gone with that boy, I wonder? You Tom!"

—MARK TWAIN, *The Adventures of Tom Sawyer*

"Well, Peter, not in sight yet?" was the question asked on May 20th, 1859, by a gentleman a little over forty, in a dusty coat and checked trousers, who came out hatless to the low porch of the posting station at S———. He was addressing his servant, a chubby young fellow, with whitish down on his chin, and little lack-lustre eyes.

—IVAN TURGENEV, *Fathers and Sons,*
trans. Constance Garnett, revised by Ralph E. Matlaw

"Ah, don't begin to fuss!" wailed Kitty; "if a woman began to worry in these days because her husband hadn't written to

The first page of the original manuscript of Virginia Woolf's *To the Lighthouse*. Woolf made many further word changes, beginning with the first line: "Yes, of course, if it's fine tomorrow." *(Henry W. and Albert A. Berg Collection, The New York Public Library, Astor, Lenox and Tilden Foundations)*

her for a fortnight—! Besides, if he'd been anywhere interesting, anywhere where the fighting was really hot, he'd have
found some way of telling me instead of just leaving it as
'Somewhere in France.' He'll be all right."

—REBECCA WEST, *The Return of the Soldier*

"What is it, what is it, Little One?"

I kneel to his level and tip his chin. Tears break from the
large brown eyes and set off down his face.

"That's why somebodies they tread my sore leg for
notheen. Somebodies."

I sit on my low chair and take him on my knee and tuck
his black head beneath my chin.

"There ... there ... look at my pretty boy."

—SYLVIA ASHTON-Warner, *Spinster*

"You won't be late?" There was anxiety in Marjorie Car-
ling's voice, there was something like entreaty

"No, I won't be late," said Walter, unhappily and guiltily
certain that he would be. Her voice annoyed him. It drawled
a little, it was too refined—even in misery.

"Not later than midnight."

—ALDOUS HUXLEY, *Point Counter Point*

"Take my camel, dear," said my aunt Dot, as she climbed
down from this animal on her return from High Mass. The
camel, a white Arabian Dhalur (single hump) from the

famous herd of the Ruola tribe, had been a parting present, its saddle-bags stuffed with low-carat gold and flashy orient gems, from a rich desert tycoon who owned a Levantine hotel near Palmyra. I always thought it to my aunt's credit that, in view of the camel's provenance, she had not named it Zenobia, Longinus, or Aurelian, as lesser women would have done; she had, instead, always called it, in a distant voice, my camel, or the camel.

—ROSE MACAULAY, *The Towers of Trebizond*

"Corruption? *I'll* tell you about corruption, sonny!" The old man glared into the flames in the fireplace and trembled all over, biting so hard on the stem of his pipe that it crackled once, sharply, like the fireplace logs. You could tell by the way he held up the stem and looked at it, it would never be the same.

—JOHN GARDNER, *October Light*

"Yes, yes, young ladies; toss your heads as much as you please; the wisest and best among you is——. But I shall not say it; for she is the only one of my class who has a particle of modesty, and I should fear, were I to name her, that she should forthwith lose that uncommon virtue which I could wish to see in you—"

"In nomine Patris, et Filii, et Spiritus Sancti," sang Costanza, with an air of effrontery.

"Amen!" exclaimed all the other girls in chorus.

—GEORGE SAND, *Consuelo*

"Don't look now," John said to his wife, "but there are a couple of old girls two tables away who are trying to hypnotise me."

Laura, quick on cue, made an elaborate pretense of yawning, then tilted her head as though searching the skies for a non-existent aircraft.

—DAPHNE DU MAURIER, *Don't Look Now*

"The Signora had no business to do it," said Miss Bartlett, "no business at all. She promised us south rooms with a view close together, instead of which here are north rooms, looking into a courtyard, and a long way apart. Oh, Lucy!"

—E. M. FORSTER, *A Room With a View*

"I wonder when in the world you're going to do anything, Rudolf?" said my brother's wife.

"My dear Rose," I answered, laying down my egg-spoon, "why in the world should I do anything? My position is a comfortable one. I have an income nearly sufficient for my wants (no one's income is ever quite sufficient, you know), I enjoy an enviable social position: I am brother to Lord Burlesdon, and brother-in-law to that charming lady, his countess. Behold, it is enough!"

—ANTHONY HOPE, *The Prisoner of Zenda*

"*Permettez-moi de vous présenter Sam McGuire,*" Charles says. Sam is standing in the doorway holding a carton of beer.

Since Sam's dog died, he has been drinking a lot of beer. It is raining, and Sam's hair streams down his face.

"Hi," Susan says without looking up.

—ANN BEATTIE, *Chilly Scenes of Winter*

"Sleep well, dear."

Noboru's mother closed his bedroom door and locked it. What would she do if there were a fire? Let him out first thing—she had promised herself that. But what if the wooden door warped in the heat or paint clogged the keyhole? The window? There was a gravel path below; besides, the second floor of this gangling house was hopelessly high.

—YUKIO MISHIMA, *The Sailor Who Fell from Grace with the Sea,* trans. John Nathan

GHOSTS

"It may be only blackmail," said the man in the taxi hopefully. The fog was like a saffron blanket soaked in ice-water. It had hung over London all day and at last was beginning to descend. The sky was yellow as a duster and the rest was a granular black, overprinted in grey and lightened by occasional slivers of bright fish colour as a policeman turned in his wet cape.

—MARGERY ALLINGHAM, *The Tiger in the Smoke*

"What's it going to be then, eh?"

There was me, that is Alex, and my three droogs, that
is Pete, Georgie, and Dim, Dim being really dim, and we
sat in the Korova Milkbar making up our rassoodocks what
to do with the evening, a flip dark chill winter bastard
though dry.

—ANTHONY BURGESS, *A Clockwork Orange*

"Now, what I want is, Facts. Teach these boys and girls
nothing but Facts. Facts alone are wanted in life. Plant nothing else, and root out everything else. You can only form the
minds of reasoning animals upon Facts; nothing else will ever
be of any service to them. This is the principle on which I
bring up my own children, and this is the principle on
which I bring up these children. Stick to Facts, sir!"

The scene was a plain, bare, monotonous vault of a
schoolroom, and the speaker's square forefinger emphasized
his observations by underscoring every sentence with a line
on the schoolmaster's sleeve.

—CHARLES DICKENS, *Hard Times*

"Is it possible to live in despair and not wish for death?" To
amuse myself, I imagined I was reading this question on a
kind of scroll that an immense bat, its wings spread like the
one in Dürer's *Melencolia,* was holding in its talons, above the
sea, as the boat rapidly approached the island of Capri.

—ALBERT MORAVIA, *1934,* trans. William Weaver

"Well, turn around, son! What a scarecrow you are! What sort of a priest's cassock have you got on? Is that the way they all dress at the Academy?"

With these words did old Bulba greet his two sons, who, after finishing their education at the Kiev Seminary, had returned home.

—NICOLAI GOGOL, *Taras Bulba,* trans. Bernard Faber

9 ❧ THE FLASHBACK

he flashback is the solution to the writer's quandary of how to arrest the reader's attention in some exciting way, and yet tell the story from its beginning. The flashback permits the author to engage the reader at one point in the character's life, and then, by suspending time, to return to a previous point, from which the story proceeds at a more leisurely pace.

Being a recollection, the flashback requires returning to a place, and the novel's beginning then becomes the description of that place. Ernest Hemingway's *A Farewell to Arms,* Truman Capote's *Breakfast at Tiffany's,* and E. L. Doctorow's *Ragtime* all begin by evoking memories of houses. Sometimes the memory is bitter; sometimes sweet and innocent, as, for instance, in Gabriel García Márquez's *One Hundred Years of Solitude*: "Many years later, as he faced the firing squad, Colonel Aureliano Buendía was to remember that distant afternoon when his father took him to discover ice." As an evocation, the flashback has the hazy romantic aura of reverie. Can any beginning surpass the poetry of Daphne du Maurier's "Last night I dreamt I went to Manderley again"? Or the simplicity of Carson McCullers' "It happened that green and crazy summer when Frankie was twelve years old"?

The flashback works because its structure is entirely familiar to us: it is the way we tell stories in our own lives. "Remember the time we found that old love letter in the trunk in the attic," "Remember the summer that strange girl nearly drowned at the lake?" Recalling the past to the present, we then return to time remembered.

From Time to Time ∾
The author remembers how it was.

Last night I dreamt I went to Manderley again. It seemed to me I stood by the iron gate leading to the drive, and for a while I could not enter for the way was barred to me. There was a padlock and a chain upon the gate. I called in my dream to the lodge-keeper, and had no answer, and peering closer through the rusted spokes of the gate I saw that the lodge was uninhabited.

—DAPHNE DU MAURIER, *Rebecca*

In the late summer of that year we lived in a house in a village that looked across the river and the plain to the mountains. In the bed of the river there were pebbles and boulders, dry and white in the sun, and the water was clear and swiftly moving and blue in the channels. Troops went by the house and down the road and the dust they raised powdered the leaves of the trees. The trunks of the trees too were dusty and the leaves fell early that year and we saw the troops marching along the road and the dust rising and leaves, stirred by the breeze, falling and the soldiers marching and afterward the road bare and white except for the leaves.

—ERNEST HEMINGWAY, *A Farewell to Arms*

In those days cheap apartments were almost impossible to find in Manhattan, so I had to move to Brooklyn. This was in 1947, and one of the pleasant features of that summer which I so vividly remember was the weather, which was sunny and mild, flower-fragrant, almost as if the days had been arrested in a seemingly perpetual springtime. I was grateful for that if for nothing else, since my youth, I felt, was at its lowest ebb.

—WILLIAM STYRON, *Sophie's Choice*

In 1902 Father built a house at the crest of the Broadview Avenue hill in New Rochelle, New York. It was a three-story brown shingle with dormers, bay windows and a screened porch. Striped awnings shaded the windows. The family took possession of this stout manse on a sunny day in

June and it seemed for some years thereafter that all their days would be warm and fair.

—E. L. DOCTOROW, *Ragtime*

In the spring of that year an epidemic of rabies broke out in Ether County, Georgia. The disease was carried principally by foxes and was reported first by farmers, who, in the months of April and May, shot more than seventy of the animals and turned them in to the county health officer in Cotton Point.

—PETE DEXTER, *Paris Trout*

It happened that green and crazy summer when Frankie was twelve years old. This was the summer when for a long time she had not been a member. She belonged to no club and was a member of nothing in the world. Frankie had become an unjoined person who hung around in doorways, and she was afraid.

—CARSON MCCULLERS, *The Member of the Wedding*

It was a queer, sultry summer, the summer they electrocuted the Rosenbergs, and I didn't know what I was doing in New York. I'm stupid about executions. The idea of being electrocuted makes me sick, and that's all there was to read about in the papers—goggle-eyed headlines staring up at me on every street corner and at the fusty, peanut-smelling mouth of every subway. It had nothing to do with me, but I couldn't help wondering what it would be like, being burned alive all along your nerves.

—SYLVIA PLATH, *The Bell Jar*

You must go back with me to the autumn of 1827. My father, as you know, was a sort of gentleman farmer in—— shire; and I, by his express desire, succeeded him in the same quiet occupation, not very willingly, for ambition urged me to higher aims, and self-conceit assured me that, in disregarding its voice, I was burying my talent in the earth, and hiding my light under a bushel.

—ANNE BRONTË, *The Tenant of Wildfell Hall*

Serene was a word you could put to Brooklyn, New York. Especially in the summer of 1912. Somber, as a word, was better. But it did not apply to Williamsburg, Brooklyn. Prairie was lovely and Shenandoah had a beautiful sound, but you couldn't fit those words into Brooklyn. Serene was the only word for it; especially on a Saturday afternoon in summer.

—BETTY SMITH, *A Tree Grows In Brooklyn*

This was where I used to come, as a child, for holidays.

As I looked out of the train window I recognized paths and tunnels among the cliffs. On some of the sheer faces sol-

diers were stretched out like specimen butterflies. The town
was, as I always remembered it, shrouded in rain.

—JOHN MORTIMER, *Charade*

I went back to the Devon School not long ago, and found it
looking oddly newer than when I was a student there fifteen
years before. It seemed more sedate than I remembered it,
more perpendicular and strait-laced, with narrower windows and shinier woodwork, as though a coat of varnish
had been put over everything for better preservation. But,
of course, fifteen years before there had been a war going
on. Perhaps the school wasn't as well kept up in those
days; perhaps varnish, along with everything else, had gone
to war.

—JOHN KNOWLES, *A Separate Peace*

When I was a small boy at the beginning of the century I
remember an old man who wore knee-breeches and worsted
stockings, and who used to hobble about the street of our
village with the help of a stick. He must have been getting
on for eighty in the year 1807, earlier than which date I suppose I can hardly remember him, for I was born in 1802. A
few white locks hung about his ears, his shoulders were bent
and his knees feeble, but he was still hale, and was much
respected in our little world of Paleham. His name was Pon-
tifex.

—SAMUEL BUTLER, *The Way of All Flesh*

When he was nearly thirteen, my brother Jem got his arm badly broken at the elbow. When it healed, and Jem's fears of never being able to play football were assuaged, he was seldom self-conscious about his injury. His left arm was somewhat shorter than his right; when he stood or walked, the back of his hand was at right angles to his body, his thumb parallel to his thigh. He couldn't have cared less, so long as he could pass and punt.

—HARPER LEE, *To Kill a Mockingbird*

The first time I saw Brenda she asked me to hold her glasses. Then she stepped out to the edge of the diving board and looked foggily into the pool; it could have been drained, myopic Brenda would never have known it. She dove beautifully, and a moment later she was swimming back to the side of the pool, her head of short-clipped auburn hair held up, straight ahead of her, as though it were a rose on a long stem. She glided to the edge and then was beside me. "Thank you," she said, her eyes watery though not from the water.

—PHILIP ROTH, *Goodbye, Columbus*

Many years later, as he faced the firing squad, Colonel Aureliano Buendía was to remember that distant afternoon when his father took him to discover ice. At that time Macondo was a village of twenty adobe houses, built on the bank of a river of clear water that ran along a bed of polished stones, which were white and enormous, like prehistoric eggs. The world was so recent that many things lacked names, and in order to indicate them it was necessary to point.

—GABRIEL GARCÍA MÁRQUEZ, *One Hundred Years of Solitude,* trans. Gregory Rabassa

I am always drawn back to places where I have lived, the houses and their neighborhoods. For instance, there is a brownstone in the East Seventies where, during the early years of the war, I had my first New York apartment. It was one room crowded with attic furniture, a sofa and fat chairs upholstered in that itchy, particular red velvet that one associates with hot days on a train. The walls were stucco, and a color rather like tobacco-spit. Everywhere, in the bathroom too, there were prints of Roman ruins freckled brown with age. The single window looked out on a fire escape. Even so, my spirits heightened whenever I felt in my pocket the key to this apartment; with all its gloom, it still was a place of my own, the first, and my books were there, and jars of pencils to sharpen, everything I needed, so I felt, to become the writer I wanted to be.

—TRUMAN CAPOTE, *Breakfast at Tiffany's*

All this happened, more or less. The war parts, anyway, are pretty much true. One guy I knew really *was* shot in Dresden for taking a teapot that wasn't his. Another guy I knew really *did* threaten to have his personal enemies killed by hired gunmen after the war. And so on. I've changed all the names.

—KURT VONNEGUT, JR., *Slaughterhouse-Five*

All of this happened while I was walking around starving in Christiania—that strange city no one escapes from until it has left its mark on him. . . .

I was lying awake in my attic room; a clock struck six somewhere below; it was fairly light already and people were beginning to move up and down the stairs. Over near the door, where my wall was papered with old issues of the *Morning Times,* I could make out a message from the Chief of Lighthouses, and just to the left of that an advertisement for fresh bread, showing a big, fat loaf: Fabian Olsen's bakery.

—KNUT HAMSUN, *Hunger,* trans. Robert Bly

Of late years, an abundant shower of curates has fallen upon the north of England: they lie very thick on the hills; every parish has one or more of them; they are young enough to be very active, and ought to be doing a great deal of good. But not of late years are we about to speak; we are going back to the beginning of this century: late years—present years are dusty, sun-burnt, hot, arid; we will evade the noon, forget it in siesta, pass the mid-day in slumber, and dream of dawn.

—CHARLOTTE BRONTË, *Shirley*

Looking back to all that has occurred to me since that eventful day, I am scarcely able to believe in the reality of my adventures. They were truly so wonderful that even now I am bewildered when I think of them.

My uncle was a German, having married my mother's sister, an Englishwoman. Being very much attached to his fatherless nephew, he invited me to study under him in his home in the fatherland. This home was in a large town, and my uncle a professor of philosophy, chemistry, geology, mineralogy, and many other ologies.

—JULES VERNE, *A Journey to the Center of the Earth*

10 ❧ THE EPISTLE

ne of the Victorians' favorite devices was the epistle, usually in the form of a letter, but sometimes written as an entry in a journal. In journal form, the epistle served much the same purpose as first person narration: it made the reader privy to the hero's deepest thoughts and secrets. The hero was less likely to be as revealing in a letter to a second character; that is, unless his whole purpose in "writing" it was to bare his feelings.

Like beginning dialogue, the opening letter or diary entry draws the reader a portrait of the character: his sensitivity or lack of it, his intelligence or stupidity, his stage of maturity, and his state of mind. The "letter of God" at the beginning of Alice Walker's *The Color Purple* is a wonderful example of character drawing without a word of description.

The letter also has a second purpose: it moves the plot.

The plot can be advanced, too, by the use of a "newspaper story" like that at the beginning of Doris Lessing's *The Grass Is Singing,* or even a public proclamation, as in William Styron's *The Confession of Nat Turner.* Used here to begin the book, it provides necessary background information, and is presented as a short preface.

Take an Epistle ⁓
A letter, a diary entry, begins the story.

3 May. Bistritz.—Left Munich at 8:35 P.M., on 1st May, arriving at Vienna early next morning; should have arrived at 6:46, but train was an hour late. Buda-Pesth seems a wonderful place, from the glimpse which I got of it from the train and the little I could walk through the streets. I feared to go very far from the station, as we arrived late and would start as near the correct time as possible.

—BRAM STOKER, *Dracula*

March 16th

A gentleman friend and I were dining at the Ritz last evening and he said that if I took a pencil and a paper and put down all of my thoughts it would make a book. This almost made me smile as what it would really make would be a whole row of encyclopediaes. I mean I seem to be thinking practically all of the time. I mean it is my favorite recreation and sometimes I sit for hours and do not seem to do anything else but think.

—ANITA LOOS, *Gentlemen Prefer Blondes*

(Autumn 1930)
From my window, the deep solemn massive street. Cellar-shops where the lamps burn all day, under the shadow of top-heavy balconied façades, dirty plaster frontages embossed with scrollwork and heraldic devices. The whole district is like this: street leading into street of houses like shabby monumental safes crammed with the tarnished valuables and second-hand furniture of a bankrupt middle class.

I am a camera with its shutter open, quite passive, recording, not thinking. Recording the man shaving at the window opposite and the woman in the kimono washing her hair. Some day, all this will have to be developed, carefully printed, fixed.

—CHRISTOPHER ISHERWOOD, *Goodbye to Berlin*

SEPTEMBER 10, 1939. I have always wanted to keep a journal, but whenever I am about to start one, I am dissuaded by the idea that it is too late. I lose heart when I think of all the fascinating things I could have described had I only begun earlier. Not that my life has been an exciting one. On the contrary, it has been very dull. But a dull life in itself may be an argument for a journal. The best way for the passive man to overtake his more active brothers is to write them up. Isn't the Sun King himself just another character in Saint-Simon's chronicle?

—LOUIS AUCHINCLOSS, *The Rector of Justin*

1968

FROM BILLY ABBOTT'S NOTEBOOK—
I AM WORTHLESS, MONIKA SAYS. SHE SAYS IT ONLY HALF-SERIOUSLY. MONIKA, ON THE OTHER HAND, IS NOT DEMONSTRABLY WORTH-LESS. BEING IN LOVE WITH HER UNDOUBTEDLY CLOUDS MY VISION OF HER. MORE ABOUT THAT LATER.

—IRWIN SHAW, *Beggarman, Thief*

progris riport 1 martch 3
    Dr. Strauss says I shoud rite down what I think and remembir and evrey thing that happins to me from now on. I dont no why but he says its importint so they will see if they can use me. I hope they use me becaus Miss Kinnian says mabye they can make me smart. I want to be smart. My name is Charlie Gordon I werk in Donners bakery where Mr Donner gives me 11 dollers a week and bred or cake if I want. I am 32 yeres old and next munth is my brithday.

—DANIEL KEYES, *Flowers for Algernon*

You better not never tell nobody but God. It'd kill your mammy.

Dear God,
I am fourteen years old. ~~I am~~ I have always been a good
girl. Maybe you can give me a sign letting me know what is
happening to me.
Last spring after little Lucious come I heard them fussing.
He was pulling on her arm. She say It too soon, Fonso, I
ain't well. Finally he leave her alone. A week go by, he
pulling on her arm again. She say Naw, I ain't gonna. Can't
you see I'm already half dead, an all of these children.
— ALICE WALKER, *The Color Purple*

(TO MONSIEUR D.R., PRÉSIDENT DU CONSEIL)

Sidi b. M. July 30, 189_.

*Yes, you were right: Michel has spoken to us, my dear brother.
The account he gave is what follows. You had asked me for it; I
promised it to you; but at the very moment I send it, I still hesitate,
and the more I read it over, the more dreadful it seems. What will
you think of our friend?*
— ANDRE GIDE, *The Immoralist*

One may as well begin with Helen's letters to her sister.

Howards End,

Tuesday.
Dearest Meg,
It isn't going to be what we expected. It is old and little, and

altogether delightful—red brick. We can scarcely pack in as it is, and the dear knows what will happen when Paul (younger son) arrives tomorrow.

—E. M. FORSTER, *Howard's End*

Libanius to Priscus   *Antioch, March [A.D.] 380*
Yesterday morning as I was about to enter the lecture hall, I was stopped by a Christian student who asked me in a voice eager with malice, "Have you heard about the Emperor Theodosius?"

I cleared my throat ready to investigate the nature of this question, but he was too quick for me. "He has been baptized a Christian."

—GORE VIDAL, *Julian*

SIDNEY SLYTER SAYS
Dreary Station Severely Damaged During Night ...
Bomber Crashes in Laundry Court ...
Fires Burning Still in Violet lane ...
Last night Blood's End was quiet; there was some activity in Highland Green; while Dreary Station took the worst of Jerry's effort. And Sidney Slyter has this to say: a beautiful afternoon, a lovely crowd, a taste of bitters, and light returning to the faces of heroic stone—one day there will be amuse-

ments everywhere good fun for our mortality, and you'll whistle and flick your cigarette into an old crater's lip and with your young woman go off to a fancy flutter at the races.

—JOHN HAWKES, *The Lime Twig*

A Great Day

FOR RAINTREE COUNTY
(Epic Fragment from the *Free Enquirer,* July 4, 1892)

Yes, Sir, here's the Glorious Fourth again. And here's our special Semicentennial Edition of the *Free Enquirer,* fifty pages crowded with memories of fifty years since we published the first copy of this newspaper in 1842. And, friends, what a half-century it has been!

—ROSS LOCKRIDGE, JR., *Raintree County*

MURDER MYSTERY
By Special Correspondent
Mary Turner, wife of Richard Turner, a farmer at Ngesi, was found murdered on the front veranda of their homestead yesterday morning. The houseboy, who has been arrested, has confessed to the crime. No motive has been discovered. It is thought he was in search of valuables.

—DORIS LESSING, *The Grass Is Singing*

11 ❦ STATEMENT OF
PHILOSOPHY

L ying beneath the active plot, the characters, and the setting of a novel is the statement that the author wishes to make. Sometimes a universal truth or a personal observation will have suggested the story, and the author sets up the novel by beginning with that thought. "It is a truth universally acknowledged, that a single man in possession of a good fortune must be in want of a wife," writes Jane Austen in *Pride and Prejudice*. And D. H. Lawrence begins *Lady Chatterley's Lover*: "Ours is essentially a tragic age, so we refuse to take it tragically." The author waxes philosophical for a moment before turning to his characters, plot, or setting. Perhaps the most eloquent and memorable example of such a statement is Dickens' brilliant opening paragraph—for it *is* an entire paragraph—to *A Tale of Two Cities*: "It was the best of times, it was the worst of times, it was the age of wisdom, it was the age of foolishness, it was the epoch of belief, it was the epoch of incredulity, it was the season of Light, it was the season of Darkness, it was the spring of hope, it was the winter of despair ..." Dickens leads us on through this catalog of antitheses, before telling us that in fact, the time he has in mind is one very much like the present.

Some of the statements presented in this chapter are profound and predictive of the story; others are merely personal observations used as starting points. All make the reader pause for a moment, reflect, and hopefully begin to nod in assent.

The Whole Truth ∿

The author sets the story with the introduction of a belief.

It is a truth universally acknowledged, that a single man in possession of a good fortune must be in want of a wife.

However little known the feelings or views of such a man may be on his first entering a neighbourhood, this truth is so well fixed in the minds of the surrounding families, that he is considered as the rightful property of someone or other of their daughters.

—JANE AUSTEN, *Pride and Prejudice*

Ours is essentially a tragic age, so we refuse to take it tragically. The cataclysm has happened, we are among the ruins, we start to build up new little habitats, to have new little hopes. It is rather hard work: there is now no smooth road into the future: but we go round, or scramble over the obsta-

Lady Chatterley's Lover
by DH Lawrence

Ours is essentially a tragic age, ~~so we won't it tragedy~~ *but we refuse* ~~oh no we won't~~ emphatically to be tragic about it.

This was Constance Chatterley's position. The war landed her in a ~~tragic~~ *dreadful* situation, and she was determined not to make a tragedy out of it.

She married Clifford Chatterley in 1917, when he was home on leave. They had a month of honeymoon, and he went back to France. In 1918 he was very badly wounded, brought home a wreck. She was twenty-three years old.

After two years, he was restored to comparative health. But the lower part of his body was paralysed for ever. He could wheel himself about in a wheeled chair, and he had a little motor attached to a bath chair, so that he could even make ~~slow~~ excursions in the grounds at home.

Clifford had suffered so much, that the capacity for suffering had to some extent left him. He remained strange and bright and cheerful, with his ruddy, quite handsome face, and his bright, ~~ordinary~~ *haunted* blue eyes. He had so nearly lost life, that what remained to him

The first pages of the first and second versions of D. H. Lawrence's *Lady Chatterley's Lover*, in original manuscript. Lawrence alters and enlarges on his opening philosophic

Lady Chatterley's Lover.

by D.H. Lawrence

Chapter I

Ours is essentially a tragic age, so we refuse to take it tragically. The cataclysm has fallen, we've got used to the ruins, and we start to build up new little habitats, new little hopes. If we can't make a road through the obstacles, we go round, or climb over the top. We've got to live, no matter how many skies have fallen. Having tragically wrung our hands, we now proceed to peel the potatoes, or to put on the wireless.

This was Constance Chatterley's position. The war landed her in a very tight situation. But she made up her mind to live and learn.

She married Clifford Chatterley in 1917, when he was home for a month on leave. They had a months honeymoon. Then he went back to Flanders. To be shipped over to England again, six months later, more or less in bits. Constance, his wife, was then twenty-three years old. and he was twenty nine.

His hold in life was marvellous. He didn't die, and the bits seemed to grow together again. For two years, he remained in the doctors hands. Then he was pronounced a cure, and could return to life again, with the lower half of his body, from the hips down, paralysed for ever.

thought, but the beginning phrase remains firm. *(Harry Ransom Humanities Research Center, The University of Texas at Austin)* cles. We've got to live, no matter how many skies have fallen.

This was more or less Constance Chatterley's position. The war had brought the roof down over her head. And she had realised that one must live and learn.

—D. H. LAWRENCE, *Lady Chatterley's Lover*

It was the best of times, it was the worst of times, it was the age of wisdom, it was the age of foolishness, it was the epoch of belief, it was the epoch of incredulity, it was the season of Light, it was the season of Darkness, it was the spring of hope, it was the winter of despair, we had everything before us, we had nothing before us, we were all going direct to Heaven, we were all going direct the other way—in short, the period was so far like the present period, that some of its noisiest authorities insisted on its being received, for good or for evil, in the superlative degree of comparison only.

—CHARLES DICKENS, *A Tale of Two Cities*

Happy families are all alike; every unhappy family is unhappy in its own way.

Everything was in confusion in the Oblonskys' house. The wife had discovered that the husband was carrying on an intrigue with a French girl, who had been a governess in their family, and she had announced to her husband that she could not go on living in the same house with him.

—COUNT LEO TOLSTOY, *Anna Karenina,*
trans. Constance Garnett

"All happy families are more or less dissimilar; all unhappy ones are more or less alike," says a great Russian writer in the beginning of a famous novel (*Anna Arkadievitch Karenina,* transfigured into English by R. G. Stonelower, Mount Tabor Ltd., 1880). That pronouncement has little if any relation to the story to be unfolded now, a family chronicle, the first part of which is, perhaps, closer to another Tolstoy work, *Detstvo i Otrochestvo (Childhood and Fatherland,* Pontius Press, 1858).
—VLADIMIR NABOKOV, *Ada or Ardor: A Family Chronicle*

Those privileged to be present at a family festival of the Forsytes have seen that charming and instructive sight—an upper middle-class family in full plumage. But whosoever of these favoured persons has possessed the gift of psychological analysis (a talent without monetary value and properly ignored by the Forsytes), has witnessed a spectacle, not only delightful in itself, but illustrative of an obscure human problem. In plainer words, he has gleaned from a gathering of this family—no branch of which had a liking for the other, between no three members of whom existed anything worthy of the name of sympathy—evidence of that mysterious concrete tenacity which renders a family so formidable a unit of society, so clear a reproduction of society in miniature.
—JOHN GALSWORTHY, *The Forsyte Saga [The Man of Property]*

Under certain circumstances there are few hours in life more agreeable than the hour dedicated to the ceremony known as afternoon tea. There are circumstances in which, whether you partake of the tea or not—some people of course never do,—the situation is in itself delightful. Those that I have in mind in beginning to unfold this simple history offered an admirable setting to an innocent pastime.

—HENRY JAMES, *The Portrait of a Lady*

A destiny that leads the English to the Dutch is strange enough; but one that leads from Epsom into Pennsylvania, and thence into the hills that shut in Altamont over the proud coral cry of the cock, and the soft stone smile of an angel, is touched by that dark miracle of chance which makes new magic in a dusty world.

Each of us is all the sums he has not counted: subtract us into nakedness and night again, and you shall see begin in Crete four thousand years ago the love that ended yesterday in Texas.

—THOMAS WOLFE, *Look Homeward, Angel*

The insuperable gap between East and West that exists in some eyes is perhaps nothing more than an optical illusion. Perhaps it is only the conventional way of expressing a popular opinion based on insufficient evidence and masquerading as a universally recognized statement of fact, for which there is no justification at all, not even the plea that it contains an element of truth.

—PIERRE BOULLE, *The Bridge Over the River Kwai,*
trans. Xan Fielding

We all seek an ideal in life. A pleasant fancy began to visit me in a certain year, that perhaps the number of human beings is few who do not find their quest at some era of life for some space more or less brief. I had certainly not found mine in youth, though the strong belief I held of its existence sufficed through all my brightest and freshest time to keep me hopeful. I had not found it in maturity. I was become resigned never to find it. I had lived certain dim years entirely tranquil and unexpectant. And now I was not sure but something was hovering round my hearth which pleased me wonderfully.

—CHARLOTTE BRONTË, *Emma*

All true histories contain instruction; though, in some, the treasure may be hard to find, and, when found, so trivial in quantity, that the dry, shrivelled kernel scarcely compensates for the trouble of cracking the nut. Whether this be the case with my history or not, I am hardly competent to judge. I sometimes think it might prove useful to some, and entertaining to others; but the world may judge for itself. Shielded by my own obscurity, and by the lapse of years, and a few fictitious names, I do not fear to venture; and will candidly lay before the public what I would not disclose to the most intimate friend.

—ANNE BRONTË, *Agnes Grey*

Not a day passes over the earth, but men and women of no note do great deeds, speak great words, and suffer noble sorrows. Of these obscure heroes, philosophers, and martyrs, the greater part will never be known till that hour, when many that are great shall be small, and the small great; but of others the world's knowledge may be said to sleep: their lives and characters lie hidden from nations in the annals that record them.

—CHARLES READE, *The Cloister and the Hearth*

Once you have given up the ghost, everything follows with dead certainty, even in the midst of chaos. From the beginning it was never anything but chaos: it was a fluid which enveloped me, which I breathed in through the gills. In the substrata, where the moon shone steady and opaque, it was smooth and fecundating; above it was a jangle and a discord. In everything I quickly saw the opposite, the contradiction, and between the real and the unreal the irony, the paradox. I was my own worst enemy.

—HENRY MILLER, *Tropic of Capricorn*

Time is not a line but a dimension, like the dimensions of space. If you can bend space you can bend time also, and if you knew enough and could move faster than light you could travel backward in time and exist in two places at once.

—MARGARET ATWOOD, *Cat's Eye*

Customs of courtship vary greatly in different times and places, but the way the thing happens to be done here and now always seems the only natural way to do it.

Marjorie's mother looked in on her sleeping daughter at half past ten of a Sunday morning with feelings of puzzlement and dread. She disapproved of everything she saw.

—HERMAN WOUK, *Marjorie Morningstar*

Love weaves its own tapestry, spins its own golden thread, with its own sweet breath breathes into being its mysteries—bucolic, lusty, gentle as the eyes of daisies or thick with pain. And out of its own music creates the flesh of our lives. If the birds sing, the nudes are not far off. Even the dialogue of the frogs is rapturous.

—JOHN HAWKES, *The Blood Oranges*

They say when trouble comes close ranks, and so the white people did. But we were not in their ranks. The Jamaican ladies had never approved of my mother, "because she pretty like pretty self" Christophine said.

She was my father's second wife, far too young for him they thought, and, worse still a Martinique girl.

—JEAN RHYS, *Wide Sargasso Sea*

The British are frequently criticized by other nations for their dislike of change, and indeed we love England for those aspects of nature and life which change the least. Here in the West Country, where I was born, men are slow of speech, tenacious of opinion, and averse—beyond their countrymen elsewhere—to innovation of any sort. The houses of my neighbors, the tenants' cottages, the very fishing boats which ply on the Bristol Channel, all conform to the patterns of a simpler age. And an old man, forty of whose three-and-seventy years have been spent afloat, may be pardoned a not unnatural tenderness toward the scenes of his youth, and a satisfaction that these scenes remain so little altered by time.

—CHARLES NORDHOFF AND JAMES NORMAN HALL,
Mutiny on the Bounty

It was a feature peculiar to the colonial wars of North America, that the toils and dangers of the wilderness were to be encountered before the adverse hosts could meet. A wide and apparently an impervious boundary of forests severed the possessions of the hostile provinces of France and England. The hardy colonist, and the trained European who fought at his side, frequently expended months in struggling against the rapids of the streams, or in effecting the rugged passes of the mountains, in quest of an opportunity to exhibit their courage in a more martial conflict.

—JAMES FENIMORE COOPER, *The Last of the Mohicans*

I have noticed that when someone asks for you on the telephone and, finding you out, leaves a message begging you to call him up the moment you come in, as it's important, the matter is more often important to him than to you. When it comes to making you a present or doing you a favour most people are able to hold their impatience within reasonable bounds.

—W. SOMERSET MAUGHAM, *Cakes and Ale*

Not the power to remember, but its very opposite, the power to forget, is a necessary condition of our existence. If the lore of the transmigration of souls is a true one, then these, between their exchange of bodies, must pass through the sea of forgetfulness. According to the Jewish view we make the transition under the overlordship of the Angel of Forgetfulness. But it sometimes happens that the Angel of Forgetfulness himself forgets to remove from our memories the records of the former world; and then our senses are haunted by fragmentary recollections of another life.

—SHOLEM ASCH, *The Nazarene*

It was one of those days when nothing happens; when the stars, who are accustomed to variety, feeling that life will be monotonous until evening, go out without employment and huddle together like chickens when the rain is going to last. There was a bit of everything in the sky. There was the sun; there was the moon, under a cover. Night and morning were both served on the same shining cloths.

—JEAN GIRAUDOUX, *Suzanne and the Pacific,*
trans. Ben Ray Redman

12 ❦ A LITTLE BACKGROUND

Sometimes as an author begins to tell a story, he realizes that in order for the reader to fully understand what he is about to relate, a certain amount of background is necessary. It may be a description of a place or an era, or the past history of a character, but its purpose is more than description, it is explanation. It gives us the information we need to knowledgeably begin the story at the point the novelist has chosen. "In the time of Spanish rule, and for many years afterwards, the town of Sulaco—the luxuriant beauty of the orange gardens bears witness to its antiquity—had never been commercially anything more important than a coasting port with a fairly large local trade in ox-hides and indigo," sets up Joseph Conrad's *Nostromo*.

A short backgrounding paragraph at the beginning of a novel is a part of the novel proper: it starts the story. However, when the backgrounding information is so extensive that it threatens to stall the story, it is often allotted to a preface. As we will see in a later chapter, the backgrounding preface is usually unconnected to the action: the story must wait.

Back up, Please ⌒
First we're given some history.

August, 1931—The port town of Veracruz is a little purgatory between land and sea for the traveler, but the people who live there are very fond of themselves and the town they have helped to make. They live as initiates in local custom reflecting their own history and temperament, and they carry on their lives of alternate violence and lethargy with a pleasurable contempt for outside opinion, founded on the charmed notion that their ways and feelings are above and beyond criticism.

—KATHERINE ANNE PORTER, *Ship of Fools*

In that pleasant district of merry England which is watered by the river Don, there extended in ancient times a large forest, covering the greater part of the beautiful hills and valleys which lie between Sheffield and the pleasant town of Doncaster. The remains of this extensive wood are still to be seen at the noble seats of Wentworth, of Wharncliffe Park, and around Rotherham. Here haunted of yore the fabulous Dragon of Wantley; here were fought many of the most

desperate battles during the civil Wars of the Roses; and here
also flourished in ancient times those bands of gallant outlaws
whose deeds have been rendered so popular in English song.

—SIR WALTER SCOTT, *Ivanhoe*

St. Botolphs was an old place, an old river town. It had been
an inland port in the great days of the Massachusetts sailing
fleets and now it was left with a factory that manufactured
table silver and a few other small industries. The natives did
not consider that it had diminished much in size or importance, but the long roster of the Civil War dead, bolted to
the cannon on the green, was a reminder of how populous
the village had been in the 1860's.

—JOHN CHEEVER, *The Wapshot Chronicle*

As, in the triumph of Christianity, the old religion lingered
latest in the country, and died out at last as but paganism—
the religion of the villagers, before the advance of the Christian Church; so, in an earlier century, it was in places remote
from town-life that the older and purer forms of paganism
itself had survived the longest. While, in Rome, new reli-
gions had arisen with bewildering complexity around the
dying old one, the earlier and simpler patriarchal religion,
"the religion of Numa," as people loved to fancy, lingered on
with little change amid the pastoral life, out of the habits and
sentiment of which so much of it had grown.

—WALTER PATER, *Marius the Epicurean*

In the days when the spinning wheels hummed busily in the farmhouses—and even great ladies, clothed in silk and thread-lace, had their toy spinning wheels of polished oak—there might be seen, in districts far away among the lanes, or deep in the bosom of the hills, certain pallid undersized men who, by the side of the brawny countryfolk, looked like the remnants of a disinherited race. The shepherd's dog barked fiercely when one of these alien-looking men appeared on the upland, dark against the early winter sunset; for what dog likes a figure bent under a heavy bag?—and these pale men rarely stirred abroad without that mysterious burden.

—GEORGE ELIOT, *Silas Marner*

In the time of Spanish rule, and for many years afterwards, the town of Sulaco—the luxuriant beauty of the orange gardens bears witness to its antiquity—had never been commercially anything more important than a coasting port with a fairly large local trade in ox-hides and indigo. The clumsy deep-sea galleons of the conquerors that, needing a brisk gale to move at all, would lie becalmed, where your modern ship built on clipper lines forges ahead by the mere flapping of her sails, had been barred out of Sulaco by the prevailing calms of its vast gulf.

—JOSEPH CONRAD, *Nostromo*

In the time before steamships, or then more frequently than now, a stroller along the docks of any considerable seaport

would occasionally have his attention arrested by a group of
bronzed mariners, man-of-war's men or merchant sailors in
holiday attire, ashore on liberty. In certain instances they
would flank, or like a bodyguard quite surround, some
superior figure of their own class, moving along with them
like Aldebaran among the lesser lights of his constellation.
That signal object was the "Handsome Sailor" of the less
prosaic time alike of the military and merchant navies.
With no perceptible trace of the vainglorious about him,
rather with the offhand unaffectedness of natural regality,
he seemed to accept the spontaneous homage of his ship-
mates.

—HERMAN MELVILLE, *Billy Budd*

About a billion years ago, long before the continents had
separated to define the ancient oceans, or their own outlines
had been determined, a small protuberance jutted out from
the northwest corner of what would later become North
America. It showed no lofty mountains or stern shorelines,
but it was firmly rooted in solid rock and would remain per-
manently attached to primordial North America.

—JAMES A. MICHENER, *Alaska*

They used to hang men at Four Turnings in the old days.
Not any more, though. Now, when a murderer pays the
penalty for his crime, he does so up at Bodmin, after fair trial

at the Assizes. That is, if the law convicts him before his own conscience kills him. It is better so. Like a surgical operation. And the body has decent burial, though a nameless grave.

—DAPHNE DU MAURIER, *My Cousin Rachel*

Some years ago a book was published under the title of *The Pilgrim's Scrip*. It consisted of a selection of original aphorisms by an anonymous gentleman, who in this bashful manner gave a bruised heart to the world.

He made no pretension to novelty. "Our new thoughts have thrilled dead bosoms," he wrote; by which avowal it may be seen that youth had manifestly gone from him, since he had ceased to be jealous of the ancients. There was a half-sigh floating through his pages for those days of intellectual coxcombry, when ideas come to us affecting the embraces of virgins, and swear to us they are ours alone, and no one else have they ever visited: and we believe them.

—GEORGE MEREDITH, *The Ordeal of Richard Feverel*

At the time of his death the name of Albert Sanger was barely known to the musical public of Great Britain. Among the very few who had heard of him there were even some who called him Sanjé, in the French manner, being disinclined to suppose that great men are occasionally born in Hammersmith.

—MARGARET KENNEDY, *The Constant Nymph*

Everyone had always said that John would be a preacher when he grew up, just like his father. It had been said so often that John, without ever thinking about it, had come to believe it himself. Not until the morning of his fourteenth birthday did he really begin to think about it, and by then it was already too late.

—JAMES BALDWIN, *Go Tell It on the Mountain*

Andrew Stace was accustomed to say, that no man had ever despised him, and no man had ever broken him in. The omission of woman from his statement was due to his omission of her from his conception of executive life. No one disputed his assertions, though the truth of the latter had afforded satisfaction to few besides himself.

—IVY COMPTON-BURNETT, *Brothers and Sisters*

The Prince had always liked his London, when it had come to him; he was one of the modern Romans who find by the Thames a more convincing image of the truth of the ancient state than any they have left by the Tiber. Brought up on the legend of the City to which the world paid tribute, he recognized in the present London much more than in contemporary Rome the real dimensions of such a case. If it was a question of an *Imperium,* he said to himself, and if one wished, as a Roman, to recover a little the sense of that, the place to do so was on London Bridge, or even, on a fine afternoon in May, at Hyde Park Corner.

—HENRY JAMES, *The Golden Bowl*

Garp's mother, Jenny Fields, was arrested in Boston in 1942 for wounding a man in a movie theater. This was shortly after the Japanese had bombed Pearl Harbor and people were being tolerant of soldiers, because suddenly everyone *was* a soldier, but Jenny Fields was quite firm in her intolerance of the behavior of men in general and soldiers in particular. In the movie theater she had to move three times, but each time the soldier moved closer to her until she was sitting against the musty wall, her view of the newsreel almost blocked by some silly colonnade, and she resolved she would not get up and move again. The soldier moved once more and sat beside her.

—JOHN IRVING, *The World According to Garp*

The Browns have become illustrious by the pen of Thackeray and the pencil of Doyle, within the memory of the young gentlemen who are now matriculating at the Universities. Notwithstanding the well-merited but late fame which has now fallen upon them, any one at all acquainted with the family must feel, that much has yet to be written and said before the British nation will be properly sensible of how much of its greatness it owes to the Browns. For centuries, in their quiet, dogged, homespun way, they have been subduing the earth in most English counties, and leaving their mark in American forests and Australian uplands. Wherever the fleets and armies of England have won renown, there stalwart sons of the Browns have done yeomen's work.

—AN OLD BOY [Thomas Hughes], *Tom Brown's School Days*

The Brangwens had lived for generations on the Marsh farm, in the meadows where the Erewash twisted sluggishly through alder trees, separating Derbyshire from Nottinghamshire. Two miles away, a church-tower stood on a hill, the houses of the little country town climbing assiduously up to it. Whenever one of the Brangwens in the fields lifted his head from his work, he saw the church-tower at Ilkeston in the empty sky. So that as he turned again to the horizontal land, he was aware of something standing above him and beyond him in the distance.

—D. H. LAWRENCE, *The Rainbow*

The family of Dashwood had been long settled in Sussex. Their estate was large, and their residence was at Norland Park, in the centre of their property, where, for many generations, they had lived in so respectable a manner, as to engage the general good opinion of their surrounding acquaintance.

—JANE AUSTEN, *Sense and Sensibility*

Major Amberson had "made a fortune" in 1873, when other people were losing fortunes, and the magnificence of the Ambersons began then. Magnificence, like the size of a fortune, is always comparative, as even Magnificent Lorenzo may now perceive, if he has happened to haunt New York in 1916; and the Ambersons were magnificent in their day and place. Their splendour lasted throughout all the years that saw their Midland town spread and darken into a city, but reached its topmost during the period when every prosperous family with children kept a Newfoundland dog.

—BOOTH TARKINGTON, *The Magnificent Ambersons*

What can you say about a twenty-five-year-old girl who died?

That she was beautiful. And brilliant. That she loved Mozart and Bach. And the Beatles. And me. Once, when she specifically lumped me with those musical types, I asked her what the order was, and she replied, smiling, "Alphabetical."

—ERICH SEGAL, *Love Story*

For the last forty years the elderly Madame Vauquer, *née* de Conflans, has kept a family boarding-house in the Rue Neuve-Sainte-Geneviève between the Latin Quarter and the Faubourg Saint-Marcel. This boarding-house, known as the Maison Vauquer, is open to men and women, young and old, and its respectability has never been questioned by anyone. All the same, no young woman has been seen there for thirty years, and if a young man stays there it is only because his family do not allow him much money. Yet in 1819, the time when this drama begins, an almost penniless girl was living there.

—HONORÉ DE BALZAC, *Old Goriot,*
trans. Marion Ayton Crawford

The first page of the original manuscript of J. M. Barrie's *The Little Minister*. In the final version, the opening line was changed to: "Long ago in the days when our caged blackbirds never saw a king's soldier without whistling impudently. . . . " *(Henry W. and Albert A. Berg Collection, The New York Public Library, Astor, Lenox and Tilden Foundations)*

As the streets that lead from the Strand to the Embankment are very narrow, it is better not to walk down them arm-in-arm. If you persist, lawyers' clerks will have to make flying leaps into the mud; young lady typists will have to fidget behind you. In the streets of London where beauty goes unregarded, eccentricity must pay the penalty, and it is better not to be very tall, to wear a long blue cloak, or to beat the air with your left hand.

—VIRGINIA WOOLF, *The Voyage Out*

It was not a *very* white jacket, but white enough, in all conscience, as the sequel will show.

The way I came by it was this.

When our frigate lay in Callao, on the coast of Peru—her last harbour in the Pacific—I found myself without a *grego,* or sailor's surtout; and as, toward the end of a three years' cruise, no pea-jackets could be had from the purser's steward, and being bound for Cape Horn, some sort of a substitute was indispensable; I employed myself, for several days, in manufacturing an outlandish garment of my own devising, to shelter me from the boisterous weather we were so soon to encounter.

—HERMAN MELVILLE, *White-Jacket*

13 ❦ The Preface

The type of preface included in this chapter is not the non-fictional, personal author's note that is meant to give the reader some insight into the writing of the novel, but the preface that is an integral part of the story. Called a preface, an introduction, a prologue or a foreword, it contributes importantly to the novel, providing the framework within which the story can be told.

As we have noted, the preface can supply the reader with the background necessary to understand the plot or the characters without slowing down the story; Chapter I begins as if the preface did not exist. A good example of this kind of preface is Stevenson's Introductory to *Weir of Hermiston*. The preface can also set up a flashback, beginning with an episode of the novel, and returning in the first chapter to a previous time. So Charles Ryder, camped with C Company on the grounds of the Brideshead estate in the Prologue of

Evelyn Waugh's *Brideshead Revisited,* is reminded of his life with Sebastian and Julia, and can begin to tell their story in Chapter I.

In some cases the preface takes the form of the faux-author's note. The preface sets up the narrator as the finder of a manuscript of memoirs, a journal, or a book, which he then begins to reveal—as written—beginning with the first chapter, as in L. P. Hartley's *The Go-Between.* Or it details the circumstances under which the "writer" was persuaded or moved to tell the story that is to follow, in his own words, as in W. H. Hudson's *Green Mansions* or Giorgio Bassani's *The Garden of the Finzi-Continis.*

What should be becoming obvious is that the preface and its subsequent first chapter can begin with any combination of the techniques we have been examining. In fact, the preface is an ingenious solution to the problem of where to start, particularly if the writer is enamoured of two "perfect" openings: with the preface, he can have them both. The preface can begin with Background, and the first chapter with the Entrance of the Hero; it can start with Something Happening and Flashback to a Setting; it can lead with a note from the Author and be followed by a First Person narrative. The combinations are, happily, endless.

The Faux-Author Preface ⌒
The "author" explains the source of the story he is about to tell.

The pages which follow have been extracted from a pile of manuscript which was apparently meant for the eye of one woman only. She seems to have been the writer's childhood's friend. They had parted as children, or very little more than children.

—JOSEPH CONRAD, First Note, *The Arrow of Gold*

Certain streets have an atmosphere of their own, a sort of universal fame and the particular affection of their citizens. One of such streets is the Cannebière, and the jest: "If Paris had a Cannebière it would be a little Marseilles" is the jocular expression of municipal pride. I, too, I have been under the spell. For me it has been a street leading into the unknown.

—Part One, *The Arrow of Gold*

This book contains the records left us by a man whom, according to the expression he often used himself, we called the Steppenwolf. Whether this manuscript needs any introductory remarks may be open to question. I, however, feel the need of adding a few pages to those of the Steppenwolf in which I try to record my recollections of him.

—HERMANN HESSE, Preface, *Steppenwolf,*
trans. Basil Creighton

The day had gone by just as days go by. I had killed it in accordance with my primitive and retiring way of life.

—Harry Haller's Records, *Steppenwolf*

Cigars had burned low, and we were beginning to sample
the disillusionment that usually afflicts old school friends
who have met again as men and found themselves with less
in common than they had believed they had. Rutherford
wrote novels; Wyland was one of the Embassy secretaries; he
had just given us dinner at Tempelhof—not very cheerfully, I
fancied, but with the equanimity which a diplomat must
always keep on tap for such occasions.
—JAMES HILTON, Prologue, *Lost Horizon*

During that third week of May the situation in Baskul had
become much worse and, on the 20th, Air Force machines
arrived by arrangement from Peshawur to evacuate the
white residents. These numbered about eighty, and most
were safely transported across the mountains in troop-
carriers. A few miscellaneous aircraft were also employed,
among them being a cabin machine lent by the Maharajah
of Chandapore.
—Chapter I, *Lost Horizon*

The past is a foreign country: they do things differently
there.
When I came upon the diary it was lying at the bottom
of a rather battered red cardboard collar-box, in which as
a small boy I kept my Eton collars. Someone, probably
my mother, had filled it with treasures dating from those days.
—L. P. HARTLEY, Prologue, *The Go-Between*

The eighth of July was a Sunday and on the following Monday I left West Hatch, the village where we lived near Salisbury, for Brandham Hall. My mother arranged that my Aunt Charlotte, a Londoner, should take me across London. Between bouts of stomach-turning trepidation I looked forward wildly to the visit.

—Chapter I, *The Go-Between*

For many years I wanted to write about the Finzi-Continis— about Micòl and Alberto, about Professor Ermanno and Signora Olga—and about all the others who inhabited or, like me, frequented the house in Corso Ercole I d'Este, in Ferrara, just before the outbreak of the last war. But the stimulus, the impulse to do it really came to me only a year ago, on a Sunday in April 1957.

—Giorgio Bassani, Prologue, *The Garden of the Finzi-Continis,* trans. William Weaver

The tomb was big, massive, really imposing: a kind of half-ancient, half-Oriental temple of the sort seen in the sets of *Aïda* and *Nabucco* in vogue in our opera houses until a few years ago.

—Part I, *The Garden of the Finzi-Continis*

About a year ago, when I was in the royal library doing research for my history of Louis XIV, I happened to come upon the *Memoirs of Monsieur d'Artagnan,* which, like most works of that time, when authors wanted to tell the truth without having to spend time in the Bastille, was printed in Amsterdam, by Pierre Rouge. The title attracted me; I took the book home, with the librarian's permission, of course, and devoured it.

—ALEXANDRE DUMAS, Preface, *The Three Musketeers*

On the first Monday of April, 1625, the market town of Meung, birthplace of the author of the *Roman de la Rose,* seemed to be in as great a turmoil as if the Huguenots had come to turn it into a second La Rochelle. A number of townsmen, seeing women running in the direction of the main street and hearing children shouting on doorsteps, hastened to put on their breastplates and, steadying their rather uncertain self-assurance with a musket or a halberd, made their way toward the inn, the Hôtellerie du Franc Meunier, in front of which a noisy, dense, and curious throng was growing larger by the minute.

—Chapter I, *The Three Musketeers*

The story of Hans Castorp, which we would here set forth, not on his own account, for in him the reader will make acquaintance with a simple-minded though pleasing young man, but for the sake of the story itself, which seems to us highly worth telling—though it must needs be borne in mind, in Hans Castorp's behalf, that it is his story, and not every story happens to everybody—this story, we say, belongs to the long ago; is already, so to speak, covered with

historic mould, and unquestionably to be presented in the
tense best suited to a narrative out of the depth of the past.

> —THOMAS MANN, Foreword, *The Magic Mountain,*
> trans. H. T. Lowe-Porter

An unassuming young man was travelling, in midsummer,
from his native city of Hamburg to Davos-Platz in the Can-
ton of the Grisons, on a three weeks' visit.

> —Chapter I, *The Magic Mountain*

It is a cause of very great regret to me that this task has taken
so much longer a time than I had expected for its comple-
tion. It is now many months—over a year, in fact—since I
wrote to Georgetown announcing my intention of publish-
ing, *in a very few months,* the whole truth about Mr. Abel.

> —W. H. HUDSON, Prologue, *Green Mansions*

Now that we are cool, he said, and regret that we hurt each
other, I am not sorry that it happened. I deserved your
reproach: a hundred times I have wished to tell you the
whole story of my travels and adventures among the savages,
and one of the reasons which prevented me was the fear that
it would have an unfortunate effect on our friendship.

> —Chapter I, *Green Mansions*

The writer, an old man with a white moustache, had some
difficulty in getting into bed. The windows of the house in

which he lived were high and he wanted to look at the trees when he awoke in the morning. A carpenter came to fix the bed so that it would be on a level with the window.

—SHERWOOD ANDERSON, The Book of the Grotesque,
Winesburg, Ohio

Upon the half decayed veranda of a small frame house that stood near the edge of a ravine near the town of Winesburg, Ohio, a fat little old man walked nervously up and down.

—Chapter I, *Winesburg, Ohio*

The Introductory Preface ∿
Someone introduces the story.

Major Victor Joppolo, U.S.A., was a good man. You will see that. It is the whole reason why I want you to know his story.
He was the Amgot officer of a small Italian town called Adano. He was more or less the American mayor after our invasion.

—JOHN HERSEY, Foreword, *A Bell for Adano*

Invasion had come to the town of Adano.

An American corporal ran tautly along the dirty Via Favemi and at the corner he threw himself down. He made certain arrangements with his light machine gun and then turned and beckoned to his friends to come forward.

—Chapter I, *A Bell for Adano*

I am an invisible man. No, I am not a spook like those who haunted Edgar Allan Poe; nor am I one of your Hollywood-movie ectoplasms. I am a man of substance, of flesh and bone, fiber and liquids—and I might even be said to possess a mind. I am invisible, understand, simply because people refuse to see me.

—RALPH ELLISON, Prologue, *Invisible Man*

It goes a long way back, some twenty years. All my life I had been looking for something, and everywhere I turned someone tried to tell me what it was. I accepted their answers too, though they were often in contradiction and even self-contradictory. I was naïve. I was looking for myself and asking everyone except myself questions which I, and only I, could answer.

—Chapter I, *Invisible Man*

What I'm going to do is to write off the story of Rick Martin's life, now that it's all over, now that Rick is washed up and gone, as they say, to his rest.

—DOROTHY BAKER, Prologue, *Young Man with a Horn*

In the first place maybe he shouldn't have got himself mixed up with negroes. It gave him a funny slant on things and he never got over it.

—Book One, *Young Man with a Horn*

This is the story—the long and true story—of one ocean,
two ships, and about a hundred and fifty men. It is a long
story because it deals with a long and brutal battle, the worst
of any war. It has two ships because one was sunk and had to
be replaced. It has a hundred and fifty men because that is a
manageable number of people to tell a story about. Above
all, it is a true story because that is the only kind worth
telling.

—NICHOLAS MONSARRAT, Before the Curtain,
The Cruel Sea

Lieutenant-Commander George Eastwood Ericson, R.N.R.,
sat in a stone cold, draughty, corrugated-iron hut beside
the fitting-out dock of Fleming's Shipyard on the River
Clyde.

—Part One, *The Cruel Sea*

The Action Preface ∼
Starting with action, we return to the beginning of the story.

When I reached C Company lines, which were at the top of
the hill, I paused and looked back at the camp, just coming
into full view below me through the grey mist of early
morning. We were leaving that day. When we marched in,
three months before, the place was under snow; now the first
leaves of spring were unfolding. I had reflected then that,

whatever scenes of desolation lay ahead of us, I never feared one more brutal than this, and I reflected now that it had no single happy memory for me.

      —EVELYN WAUGH, Prologue, *Brideshead Revisited*

"I have been here before," I said; I had been there before; first with Sebastian more than twenty years ago on a cloudless day in June, when the ditches were creamy with meadowsweet and the air heavy with all the scents of summer; it was a day of peculiar splendour, and though I had been there so often, in so many moods, it was to that first visit that my heart returned on this, my latest.

      —Book One, *Brideshead Revisited*

Dirk Struan *came up onto the quarterdeck of the flagship H.M.S. Vengeance, and strode for the gangway. The 74-gun ship of the line was anchored half a mile off the island. Surrounding her were the rest of the fleet's warships, the troopships of the expeditionary force, and the merchantmen and opium clippers of the China traders.*

      It was dawn—a drab, chill Tuesday—January 26th, 1841.

      —JAMES CLAVELL, [prologue], *Tai-Pan*

"A pox on this stinking island," Brock said, staring around the beach and up at the mountains. "The whole of China at our feets and all we takes be this barren, sodding rock."

      —Chapter I, *Tai-Pan*

The small room was warm and moist. Furious blasts of thunder made the window-panes rattle and lightning seemed to streak through the room itself. No one had dared say what each was thinking—that this storm, violent even for mid-March, must be an evil omen.

          —KATHLEEN WINSOR, Prologue, *Forever Amber*

Marygreen did not change in sixteen years. It had changed little enough in the past two hundred.

          —Chapter One, *Forever Amber*

One summer evening in the year 1848, three Cardinals and a missionary Bishop from America were dining together in the gardens of a villa in the Sabine hills, overlooking Rome. The villa was famous for the fine view from its terrace. The hidden garden in which the four men sat at table lay some twenty feet below the south end of this terrace, and was a mere shelf of rock, overhanging a steep declivity planted with vineyards.

          — WILLA CATHER, Prologue: At Rome, *Death Comes for the Archbishop*

One afternoon in the autumn of 1851 a solitary horseman, followed by a pack-mule, was pushing through an arid stretch of country somewhere in central New Mexico. He had lost his way, and was trying to get back to the trail, with only his compass and his sense of direction for guides.

          —Book One, *Death Comes for the Archbishop*

More Prefaces ~
A variety of openings.

Now, in the waning days of the second World War, this ship lies at anchor in the glassy bay of one of the back islands of the Pacific. It is a Navy cargo ship. You know it as a cargo ship by the five yawning hatches, by the house amidships, by the booms that bristle from the masts like mechanical arms. You know it as a Navy ship by the color (dark, dull blue), by the white numbers painted on the bow, and unfailingly by the thin ribbon of the commission pennant flying from the mainmast. In the Navy Register, this ship is listed as the *Reluctant*. Its crew never refer to it by name: to them it is always "this bucket."

—THOMAS HEGGEN, Introduction, *Mr. Roberts*

There were fourteen officers on the *Reluctant* and all of them were Reserves.

—Chapter I, *Mr. Roberts*

About fifteen miles above New Orleans the river goes very slowly. It has broadened out there until it is almost a sea and the water is yellow with the mud of half a continent. Where the sun strikes it, it is golden.

At night the water talks with dark voices. It goes whispering down past the Natchez Trace, past Ormand until it reaches the old D'Estrehan place, and flows by that singing. But when it passes Harrow, it is silent. Men say that it is because the river is so broad here that you cannot hear the sound of the waters. Scientists say it is the shape of the channel. But it is as broad by Ormand and D'Estrehan. Yet before Harrow in the night it is silent.

—FRANK YERBY, [prologue], *The Foxes of Harrow*

The *Prairie Belle* came nuzzling up to the bar. The big side wheels slowed and the white boiling of the water stopped.

—Chapter I, *The Foxes of Harrow*

The artist is the creator of beautiful things.
To reveal art and conceal the artist is art's aim.
The critic is he who can translate into another manner or a new material his impression of beautiful things.
 The highest as the lowest form of criticism is a mode of
 autobiography.
Those who find ugly meanings in beautiful things are corrupt without being charming. This is a fault.
 Those who find beautiful meanings in beautiful
 things are the cultivated. For these there is hope....
—OSCAR WILDE, The Preface, *The Picture of Dorian Gray*

The studio was filled with the rich odour of roses, and when the light summer wind stirred amidst the trees of the garden there came through the open door the heavy scent of the lilac, or the more delicate perfume of the pink-flowering thorn.

—Chapter I, *The Picture of Dorian Gray*

Who that cares much to know the history of man, and how the mysterious mixture behaves under the varying experiments of Time, has not dwelt, at least briefly, on the life of Saint Theresa, has not smiled with some gentleness at the thought of the little girl walking forth one morning hand in hand with her still smaller brother to go and seek martyrdom in the country of the Moors?

—GEORGE ELIOT, Prelude, *Middlemarch*

Miss Brooke had that kind of beauty which seems to be thrown into relief by poor dress. Her hand and wrist were so finely formed that she could wear sleeves not less bare of style than those in which the blessed Virgin appeared to Italian painters; and her profile as well as her stature and bearing seemed to gain the more dignity from her plain garments, which by the side of provincial fashion gave her the impressiveness of a fine quotation from the Bible—or from one of our elder poets—in a paragraph of today's newspaper.

—Chapter I, *Middlemarch*

We are talking now of summer evenings in Knoxville, Tennessee in the time that I lived there so successfully disguised to myself as a child. It was a little bit mixed sort of block, fairly solidly lower middle class, with one or two juts apiece on either side of that.

—JAMES AGEE, Knoxville: Summer, 1915*,
A Death in the Family

*Presented as a preface in the posthumous printing of the book on the premise that the editors would have urged him to do so.

At supper that night, as many times before, his father said,
"Well, spose we go to the picture show."

"Oh, Jay!" his mother said. "That horrid little man!"

"What's wrong with him?" his father asked, not because
he didn't know what she would say, but so she would say it.

"He's so *nasty!*" she said, as she always did. "So *vulgar!*
With his nasty little cane; hooking up skirts and things, and
that nasty little walk!"

—Chapter I, A Death in the Family

14 ❧ BREVITY COUNTS

he dramatically-short sentence seems such a modern technique that it comes as something of a revelation to open *Bleak House* and read: "London. Michaelmas Term lately over, and the Lord Chancellor sitting in Lincoln's Inn Hall. Implacable November weather." But then, Dickens was endlessly inventive. It is almost more unusual to find an Edwardian, like Hugh Walpole, so enamored with the brief, declarative sentence that he used it again and again. "Robin Trojan was waiting for his father," begins *The Wooden Horse*; "Young Cole, quivering with pride, surveyed the room," *Jeremy at Crale*; and "The fog had swallowed up the house, and the house had submitted," *The Green Mirror*.

The three- or four-word sentence gives a novel a fast start. It sets a pace and a rhythm. And it has all the impact of understatement. "Mother died today," begins Albert Camus's

The Stranger, and we are shocked, both by the abruptness of the disclosure, and the narrator's matter-of-factness. "They're out there," opens Ken Kesey's *One Flew Over the Cuckoo's Nest,* and three carefully-chosen words reveal all the narrator's paranoia. "Nobody could sleep," writes Norman Mailer in *The Naked and the Dead,* and we feel the quiet panic of troops facing the unknowable.

Perhaps more than any other technique, the short first sentence must be *exactly* right. Like a line of poetry—and each of the first lines quoted above easily could be the start of a poem—every single word counts, and the combination of those few carefully-chosen words is extremely powerful. For the novelist troubled by the wordiness of a beginning description of setting or character, three little words might say it all.

Short and Sweet ∿
The well-chosen word or two.

I was born. It was born. So it began. It continues. It will outlive me. People whisper, stare, giggle. Their eternal privilege. My eternal curse.

—JOYCE CAROL OATES, *The Assassins*

London. Michaelmas Term lately over, and the Lord Chancellor sitting in Lincoln's Inn Hall. Implacable November weather. As much mud in the streets, as if the waters had but newly retired from the face of the earth, and it would not be wonderful to meet a Megalosaurus, forty feet long or so, waddling like an elephantine lizard up Holborn Hill.

—CHARLES DICKENS, *Bleak House*

Mother died today. Or, maybe, yesterday; I can't be sure. The telegram from the Home says: YOUR MOTHER PASSED AWAY. FUNERAL TOMORROW. DEEP SYMPATHY. Which leaves the matter doubtful; it could have been yesterday.

—ALBERT CAMUS, *The Stranger,* trans. Stuart Gilbert

I am in my mother's room. It's I who live there now. I don't know how I got there. Perhaps in an ambulance, certainly a vehicle of some kind. I was helped. I'd never have got there alone. There's this man who comes every week. Perhaps I got here thanks to him. He says not. He gives me money and takes away the pages. So many pages, so much money. Yes, I work now, a little like I used to, except that I don't know how to work any more.

—SAMUEL BECKETT, *Molloy,*
trans. Patrick Bowles in collaboration with the author

Brrrrrrriiiiiiiiiiiiiiiiiiiinng!
    An alarm clock clanged in the dark and silent room. A bed spring creaked. A woman's voice sang out impatiently:

"Bigger, shut that thing off!"

—RICHARD WRIGHT, *Native Son*

It was Wang Lung's marriage day. At first, opening his eyes in
the blackness of the curtains about his bed, he could not
think why the dawn seemed different from any other.

—PEARL S. BUCK, *The Good Earth*

They're out there.

Black boys in white suits up before me to commit sex acts
in the hall and get it mopped up before I can catch them.

They're mopping when I come out the dorm, all three of
them sulky and hating everything, the time of day, the place
they're at here, the people they got to work around. When
they hate like this, better if they don't see me.

—KEN KESEY, *One Flew Over the Cuckoo's Nest*

Dusk—of a summer night.

And the tall walls of the commercial heart of an American
city of perhaps 400,000 inhabitants—such walls as in time
may linger as a mere fable.

—THEODORE DREISER, *An American Tragedy*

124 was spiteful. Full of a baby's venom. The women in the
house knew it and so did the children. For years each put up

with the spite in his own way, but by 1873 Sethe and her
daughter Denver were its only victims.
—TONI MORRISON, *Beloved*

We are at rest five miles behind the front. Yesterday we were
relieved, and now our bellies are full of beef and haricot
beans. We are satisfied and at peace. Each man has another
mess-tin full for the evening; and, what is more, there is a
double ration of sausage and bread. That puts a man in fine
trim. We have not had such luck as this for a long time.
—ERICH MARIA REMARQUE, *All Quiet on the Western Front,*
trans. A. W. Wheen

Nobody could sleep. When morning came, assault craft
would be lowered and a first wave of troops would ride
through the surf and charge ashore on the beach at
Anopopei. All over the ship, all through the convoy, there
was a knowledge that in a few hours some of them were
going to be dead.
—NORMAN MAILER, *The Naked and the Dead*

It was love at first sight.
    The first time Yossarian saw the chaplain he fell madly in
love with him.
    Yossarian was in the hospital with a pain in his liver that

fell just short of being jaundice. The doctors were puzzled by
the fact that it wasn't quite jaundice. If it became jaundice
they could treat it. If it didn't become jaundice and went
away they could discharge him. But this just being short of
jaundice all the time confused them.

—JOSEPH HELLER, *Catch-22*

It was in 1927 or 1928. I have no memory for dates and I am
not one of those who keep a careful record of their doings, a
habit that is not uncommon in our profession and that has
proved of considerable use and even profit to some people.
And it was only quite recently that I remembered the notebooks in which my wife, for a long time without my knowledge and indeed behind my back, had stuck any newspaper
stories that referred to me.

—GEORGES SIMENON, *Maigret's Memoirs*

Howard Roark laughed.
    He stood naked at the edge of a cliff. The lake lay far
below him. A frozen explosion of granite burst in flight to
the sky over motionless water. The water seemed immov-
able, the stone—flowing. The stone had the stillness of one
brief moment in battle when thrust meets thrust and the
currents are held in a pause more dynamic than motion. The
stone glowed, wet with sunrays.

—AYN RAND, *The Fountainhead*

I

THE TEXAN)see Lower

It was love at first sight.

The first time Yossarian saw the chaplain he fell madly in love with him. Yossarian

He was in the hospital, ~~somebody that was~~ with a pain in his liver that fell just short of being jaundice. The doctors were puzzled by the fact that it wasn't quite jaundice. If it became jaundice they could treat it. If it didn't become jaundice and went away they could discharge him. But this just being short of jaundice all the time ~~only~~ confused them.

Each morning they came around, three brisk and serious men with efficient mouths and inefficient eyes, accompanied by brisk and serious Nurse Duckett, one of the ward nurses who didn't like Yossarian. They read the chart at the foot of the bed and ~~then~~ asked impatiently about the pain. They seemed irritated when he told them it was exactly the same.

"Still no movement?" the full colonel demanded.

The doctors exchanged a look when he shook his head.

"Give him another pill."

First page of the original manuscript of Joseph Heller's *Catch-22*. *(Joseph Heller Collection, Brandeis University Library, Special Collections Department)*

I am living at the Villa Borghese. There is not a crumb of dirt anywhere, nor a chair misplaced. We are all alone here and we are dead.

—HENRY MILLER, *Tropic of Cancer*

It was a pleasure to burn.

It was a special pleasure to see things eaten, to see things blackened and *changed*. With the brass nozzle in his fists, with this great python spitting its venomous kerosene upon the world, the blood pounded in his head, and his hands were the hands of some amazing conductor playing all the symphonies of blazing and burning to bring down the tatters and charcoal ruins of history. With his symbolic helmet numbered 451 on his stolid head, and his eyes all orange flame with the thought of what came next, he flicked the igniter and the house jumped up in a gorging fire that burned the evening sky red and yellow and black.

—RAY BRADBURY, *Fahrenheit 451*

The captain never drank. Yet, toward nightfall in that smoke-colored season between Indian summer and December's first true snow, he would sometimes feel half drunken. He would hang his coat neatly over the back of his chair in the leaden station-house twilight, say he was beat from lack of sleep and lay his head across his arms upon the query-room desk.

—NELSON ALGREN, *The Man With the Golden Arm*

Nunc et in hora mortis nostrae. Amen. The daily recital of the Rosary was over. For half an hour the steady voice of the Prince had recalled the Glorious and the Sorrowful Mysteries; for half an hour other voices had interwoven a lilting hum from which, now and again, would chime some unlikely word: love, virginity, death; and during that hum the whole aspect of the rococo drawing room seemed to change; even the parrots spreading iridescent wings over the silken walls appeared abashed; even the Magdalen between the two windows looked a penitent and not just a handsome blonde lost in some dubious daydream, as she usually was.

—GIUSEPPE DI LAMPEDUSA, *The Leopard,*
trans. Archibald Colquhoun

Eberlin ate alone as usual. Returning to his apartment at about six o'clock, he would shower in silence, change into something less comfortable, and sit down to a dinner-for-one prepared by an aged, yet untalkative, valet who let himself in at four o'clock every afternoon and let himself out at eight o'clock every evening.

—DEREK MARLOWE, *A Dandy in Aspic*

The moving was over and done. Professor St. Peter was alone in the dismantled house where he had lived ever since his marriage, where he had worked out his career and brought up his two daughters. It was almost as ugly as it is possible for a house to be; square, three stories in height, painted the colour of ashes—the front porch just too narrow for comfort, with a slanting floor and sagging steps.

—WILLA CATHER, *The Professor's House*

The position at the moment is as follows. I joined the gastronomic cruise at Venice, as planned, and the *Polyolbion* is now throbbing south-east in glorious summer Adriatic weather. Everything at Pulj in in order. D.R. arrived there three days ago to take over, and it was good to have a large vinous night and talk about old adventures. I am well, fit, except for my two chronic diseases of gluttony and satyriasis which, anyway, continue to cancel each other out.

—ANTHONY BURGESS, *Tremor of Intent*

I am ill; I am full of spleen and repellent. I conceive there to be something wrong with my liver, for I cannot even think for the aching of my head. Yet what my complaint is I do not know. Medicine I cannot, I never could, take, although for medicine and doctors I have much reverence. Also, I am extremely superstitious: which, it may be, is why I cherish such a respect for the medical profession. I am well-educated, and therefore might have risen superior to such fancies, yet of them I am full to the core.

—FYODOR DOSTOYEVSKY, *Letters from the Underworld,*
trans. C. J. Hogarth

What a grand guy. Sometimes he used to sneak a slug of whiskey in the forenoon, against doctor's orders. "What I like about this Daylight Saving, you don't have to wait so long for a drink." Once and a while, when I'm fixing in front of the glass I give myself a wink, I can catch just a shadow of that mischief look of his when he took the bottle from the cupboard. He said "Rum, Rheumatism and Rebellion" as he felt the stuff warm up his giblets. That wasn't a bad summary of his troubles.

—CHRISTOPHER MORLEY, *Kitty Foyle*

A nurse held the door open for them. Judge McKelva going first, then his daughter Laurel, then his wife Fay, they walked into the windowless room where the doctor would make his examination. Judge McKelva was a tall, heavy man of seventy-one who customarily wore his glasses on a ribbon. Holding them in his hand now, he sat on the raised, thronelike chair above the doctor's stool, flanked by Laurel on one side and Fay on the other.

—EUDORA WELTY, *The Optimist's Daughter*

Should he try to raise the mosquito-netting? Or should he strike through it? Ch'en was torn by anguish: he was sure of himself, yet at the moment he could feel nothing but bewilderment—his eyes riveted to the mass of white gauze that hung from the ceiling over a body less visible than a shadow,

and from which emerged only that foot half-turned in sleep,
yet living—human flesh.

—ANDRÉ MALRAUX, *Man's Fate,*
trans. Haakon M. Chevalier

The window was open. The bouquet of tulips and roses,
against the blue of the sky and the light summer air, reminded her of Matisse, and even the yellow petals falling on the
window-ledge seemed to arrange themselves gracefully for a
master's brush. Lady L. hated yellow and she wondered how
the flowers had found their way into the Ming vase. There
had been a time when every bouquet in the house had first
to be presented to her for inspection and approval.

—ROMAIN GARY, *Lady L*

A squat grey building of only thirty-four stories. Over the
main entrance the words, CENTRAL LONDON
HATCHERY AND CONDITIONING CENTRE, and, in
a shield, the World State's motto, COMMUNITY, IDEN-
TITY, STABILITY.

—ALDOUS HUXLEY, *Brave New World*

A man with binoculars. That is how it began: with a man
standing by the side of the road, on a crest overlooking a
small Arizona town, on a winter night.

Lieutenant Roger Shawn must have found the binoculars difficult. The metal would be cold, and he would be clumsy in his fur parka and heavy gloves.

—MICHAEL CRICHTON, *The Andromeda Strain*

I get the willies when I see closed doors. Even at work, where I am doing so well now, the sight of a closed door is sometimes enough to make me dread that something horrible is happening behind it, something that is going to affect me adversely; if I am tired and dejected from a night of lies or booze or sex or just plain nerves and insomnia, I can almost smell the disaster mounting invisibly and flooding out toward me through the frosted glass panes. My hands may perspire, and my voice may come out strange. I wonder why.

Something must have happened to me sometime.

—JOSEPH HELLER, *Something Happened*

The express letter came late in the afternoon.

I was standing comfortably with Matron Müller on the terrace of the clinic, putting on my usual act of kindly interest as the children packed into the big green departure coach that would take them through the mountains by the Echberg Pass to Basle for the chartered night flight back to Leeds.

—A. J. CRONIN, *A Pocketful of Rye*

15 ❦ BREVITY DOESN'T COUNT

T. E. Lawrence, acknowledging in an author's note to *The Seven Pillars of Wisdom* the many "suggestions" Charlotte and Bernard Shaw had made in regards to his masterpiece (Shaw had actually edited the book at Lawrence's request), also thanked them for "all the present semicolons." Shaw's writing is a study in the proper use of the semicolon, and, despite H. G. Wells's attempts to introduce him to the dash, he never abandoned it. Both the semicolon and the dash, of course, allow the writer to combine two or more independent thoughts that could otherwise have stood on their own as shorter sentences. They give a sentence enhanced emphasis, especially if the second part contradicts the first. They also sometimes give it a breathtaking length.

Although Henry James immediately comes to mind when we think about 100+-word sentences, he was certainly not alone in his longwindedness. (Did people speak then as they wrote?) The Victorian and Edwardian novel abounds in labyrinthian sentences that might more properly be called paragraphs. However, prodigious length did not necessarily presume dullness. The beginning sentence-paragraph of Jane Austen's *Persuasion,* with its multiple sprinkling of semicolons, is as witty as it is astute, and requires no effort of concentration at all to follow its connected clauses.

Time and stylistic changes have altered the carefully constructed, logically sequenced Victorian sentence to a twentieth century version that is free-form and almost stream of consciousness. A sentence like Joyce Carol Oates's 213-word opening to *Bellefleur does* require more concentration, but if we stay with it, by the end of the paragraph we are left with a good feeling for the book's rhythm and tone, and an initial insight into the characters.

One Hundred and Counting ∾
The 100+-word sentence.

The young man walks fast by himself through the crowd that thins into the night streets; feet are tired from hours of walking; eyes greedy for warm curve of faces, answering flicker of eyes, the set of a head, the lift of a shoulder, the way hands spread and clench; blood tingles with wants; mind is a beehive of hopes buzzing and stinging; muscles ache for the knowledge of jobs, for the roadmender's pick and shovel work, the fisherman's knack with a hook when he hauls on the slithery net from the rail of the lurching trawler, the swing of the bridgeman's arm as he slings down the whitehot rivet, the engineer's slow grip wise on the throttle, the dirt-farmer's use of his whole body when, whoaing the mules, he yanks the plow from the furrow. The young man walks by himself searching through the crowd with greedy eyes, greedy ears taut to hear, by himself, alone.

—JOHN DOS PASSOS, *U.S.A.*

It was many years ago in that dark, chaotic, unfathomable pool of time before Germaine's birth (nearly twelve months before her birth), on a night in late September stirred by innumerable frenzied winds, like spirits contending with one another—now plaintively, now angrily, now with a subtle cellolike delicacy capable of making the flesh rise on one's arms and neck—a night so sulfurous, so restless, so swollen with inarticulate longing that Leah and Gideon Bellefleur in their enormous bed quarreled once again, brought to tears because their love was too ravenous to be contained by their mere mortal bodies; and their groping, careless, anguished words were like strips of raw silk rubbed violently together (for each was convinced that the other did not, *could* not, be equal to his love—Leah doubted that any man was capable of a love so profound it could lie silent, like a forest pond; Gideon doubted that any woman was capable of comprehending the nature of a man's passion, which might tear through him, rendering him broken and exhausted, as vulnerable as a small child): it was on this tumultuous rain-lashed night that Mahalaleel came to Bellefleur Manor on the western shore of the great Lake Noir, where he was to stay for nearly five years.

—JOYCE CAROL OATES, *Bellefleur*

He had to have planned it because when we drove onto the dock the boat was there and the engine was running and you could see the water churning up phosphorescence in the river, which was the only light there was because there was no moon, nor no electric light either in the shack where the dockmaster should have been sitting, nor on the boat itself, and certainly not from the car, yet everyone knew where everything was, and when the big Packard came down the ramp Mickey the driver braked it so that the wheels hardly rattled the boards, and when he pulled up alongside the gangway the doors were already open and they hustled Bo and the girl upside before they even made a shadow in all that darkness.

—E. L. DOCTOROW, *Billy Bathgate*

Among other public buildings in a certain town, which for many reasons it will be prudent to refrain from mentioning, and to which I will assign no fictitious name, there is one anciently common to most towns, great or small: to wit, a workhouse; and in this workhouse was born; on a day and date which I need not trouble myself to repeat, inasmuch as it can be of no possible consequence to the reader, in this

stage of the business at all events; the item of mortality
whose name is prefixed to the head of this chapter.

—CHARLES DICKENS, *Oliver Twist*

In the last years of the Seventeenth Century there was to be
found among the fops and fools of the London coffee-houses
one rangy, gangling flitch called Ebenezer Cooke, more
ambitious than talented, and yet more talented than prudent,
who, like his friends-in-folly, all of whom were supposed to
be educating at Oxford or Cambridge, had found the sound
of Mother English more fun to game with than her sense to
labor over, and so rather than applying himself to the pains of
scholarship, had learned the knack of versifying, and ground
out quires of couplets after the fashion of the day, afroth with
Joves and *Jupiters,* aclang with jarring rhymes, and string-taut
with similes stretched to the snapping-point.

—JOHN BARTH, *The Sot-Weed Factor*

As no lady or gentleman, with any claims to polite breeding,
can possibly sympathise with the Chuzzlewit Family without
being first assured of the extreme antiquity of the race, it is a
great satisfaction to know that it undoubtedly descended in a
direct line from Adam and Eve; and was, in the very earliest
times, closely connected with the agricultural interest. If it
should ever be urged by grudging and malicious persons,
that a Chuzzlewit, in any period of the family history, displayed an overweening amount of family pride, surely the

weakness will be considered not only pardonable but laudable, when the immense superiority of the house to the rest
of mankind, in respect of this its ancient origin, is taken into
account.

—CHARLES DICKENS, *Martin Chuzzlewit*

From a little after two oclock until almost sundown of the
long still hot weary dead September afternoon they sat in
what Miss Coldfield still called the office because her father
had called it that—a dim hot airless room with the blinds all
closed and fastened for forty-three summers because when
she was a girl someone had believed that light and moving
air carried heat and that dark was always cooler, and which
(as the sun shone fuller and fuller on that side of the house)
became latticed with yellow slashes full of dust motes which
Quentin thought of as being flecks of the dead old dried
paint itself blown inward from the scaling blinds as wind
might have blown them.

—WILLIAM FAULKNER, *Absalom, Absalom!*

I, Tiberius Claudius Drusus Nero Germanicus This-that-
and-the-other (for I shall not trouble you yet with all my
titles) who was once, and not so long ago either, known to
my friends and relatives and associates as "Claudius the
Idiot," or "That Claudius," or "Claudius the Stammerer," or
"Clau-Clau-Claudius" or at best as "Poor Uncle Claudius,"
am now about to write this strange history of my life; start-

ing from my earliest childhood and continuing year by year until I reach the fateful point of change where, some eight years ago, at the age of fifty-one, I suddenly found myself caught in what I may call the "golden predicament" from which I have never since become disentangled.

—ROBERT GRAVES, *I, Claudius*

Sir Walter Elliot, of Kellynch Hall, in Somersetshire, was a man who, for his own amusement, never took up any book but the Baronetage; there he found occupation for an idle hour, and consolation in a distressed one; there his faculties were roused into admiration and respect by contemplating the limited remnant of the earliest patents; there any unwelcome sensations arising from domestic affairs changed naturally into pity and contempt as he turned over the almost endless creations of the last century; and there, if every other leaf were powerless, he could read his own history with an interest which never failed.

—JANE AUSTEN, *Persuasion*

16 ❦ Hardy, Hemingway, and Dickens

o two writers could be more different or representative of their ages than Thomas Hardy and
Ernest Hemingway. Where Hardy's sentences are
carefully literate, Hemingway's are coolly blunt.
Where Hardy excelled in the sensitive depiction of noble
women, Hemingway preferred painting men of machismo.
Where Hardy embraced the quiet countryside in which he
was born, Hemingway rejected his Illinois roots for the
color, the excitement, the danger of the world.

What they shared, despite wildly divergent styles, was a
reality, sometimes unlovely, but always true. Each of them
came unschooled to novelwriting—Hardy from the study of
architecture, Hemingway from journalism—finding their
way story by story. Although we have already seen some of
the beginnings of these novels in the preceding chapters, let
us now trace them chronologically.

Thomas Hardy began with a melodramatic novel called *Desperate Remedies,* published anonymously in 1871. Heavily influenced by the style of the time, he composed an opening that was typical of the Victorians, introducing his hero and heroine immediately, if intricately. One wonders whether even he suspected what "chain of circumstances" would ensue in a plot full of the coincidences that strain the belief of so many Hardy readers.

> In the long and intricately inwrought chain of circumstance which renders worthy of record some experiences of Cytherea Graye, Edward Springrove, and others, the first event directly influencing the issue was a Christmas visit.
>
> In the above-mentioned year, 1835, Ambrose Graye, a young architect who had just begun the practice of his profession in the midland town of Hocbridge, to the north of Christminster, went to London to spend the Christmas holidays with a friend who lived in Bloomsbury. They had gone up to Cambridge in the same year, and, after graduating together, Huntway, the friend, had taken orders.

Criticized for the improbability of his plot, Hardy retreated in 1872 to a simple pastoral love story, *Under the Greenwood Tree.* The first sentence, presenting a statement of naturalist philosophy, rings particularly true.

> To dwellers in a wood almost every species of tree has its voice as well as its feature. At the passing of the breeze the fir-trees sob and moan no less distinctly than they rock; the

holly whistles as it battles with itself; the ash hisses amid its quiverings; the beech rustles while its flat boughs rise and fall. And winter, which modifies the note of such trees as shed their leaves, does not destroy its individuality.

On a cold and starry Christmas-eve within living memory, a man was passing up a lane near Mellstock Cross, in the darkness of a plantation that whispered thus distinctively to his intelligence.

A Pair of Blue Eyes (1873), as we have noted before, was based on Hardy's courtship of his first wife, Emma, and quite understandably begins with a description of her fictional counterpart.

Elfride Swancourt was a girl whose emotions lay very near the surface. Their nature more precisely, and as modified by the creeping hours of time, was known only to those who watched the circumstances of her history.

Personally, she was the combination of very interesting particulars, whose rarity, however, lay in the combination itself rather than in the individual elements combined.

In 1874, in *Far from the Madding Crowd,* Hardy set a love story against the lush Dorset background of ancient hill forts, Jacobean farm houses, and harvest time. The first of his novels to give the name "Wessex" to his "dream-country," it was also the first to carry his name. The book breathes reality into strong characters, beginning with a description of Gabriel Oak, the replica of a farmer Hardy knew in Dorset, who is especially well-drawn.

When Farmer Oak smiled, the corners of his mouth spread till they were within an unimportant distance of his ears, his eyes were reduced to mere chinks, and diverging wrinkles appeared round them, extending upon his countenance like the rays in a rudimentary sketch of the rising sun.

His Christian name was Gabriel, and on working days he was a young man of sound judgment, easy motions, proper dress, and general good character. On Sundays he was a man of misty views, rather given to postponing, and hampered by his best clothes and umbrella: upon the whole, one who felt himself to occupy morally that vast middle space of Laodicean neutrality which lay between the Communion people of the parish and the drunken section,— that is, he went to church, but yawned privately by the time the congregation reached the Nicene creed, and thought of what there would be for dinner when he meant to be listening to the sermon.

Hardy's next novel, *The Hand of Ethelberta* (1876), which he called a comedy, was a disappointment to readers who had welcomed *Far from the Madding Crowd*. *Ethelberta* also begins with a description of its heroine.

Young Mrs. Petherwin stepped from the door of an old and well-appointed inn in a Wessex town to take a country walk. By her look and carriage she appeared to belong to that gentle order of society which has no worldly sorrow except when its jewellery gets stolen; but, as a fact not generally known, her claim to distinction was rather one of brains than of blood. She was the daughter of a gentleman who lived in a large house not his own, and she began life as a baby christened Ethelberta after an infant of title who does not come into the story at all, having merely furnished Ethelberta's mother with a subject of contemplation.

The Return of the Native two years later assumed a more somber note, that Hardy personified in the wild place he called Egdon Heath. The first sentence sets not only the scene, but the eerie tone of the book.

A Saturday afternoon in November was approaching the time of twilight, and the vast tract of unenclosed wild known as Egdon Heath embrowned itself moment by moment. Overhead the hollow stretch of whitish cloud shutting out the sky was as a tent which had the whole heath for its floor.

The heaven being spread with this pallid screen and the earth with the darkest vegetation, their meeting-line at the horizon was clearly marked. In such contrast the heath wore the appearance of an instalment of night which had taken up its place before its astronomical hour was come: darkness had to a great extent arrived hereon, while day stood distinct in the sky.

By 1880, with the success of *The Return of the Native* behind him, Hardy felt confident enough to write a novel on a subject that was to fascinate him all his life: Napoleon, and the West Country's preparations to resist the threatened

French invasion of England. The first sentence establishes the time period of *The Trumpet Major,* into which Hardy also introduced the Battle of Trafalgar, and his namesake and ancestor, Captain Thomas Hardy.

In the days of high-waisted and muslin-gowned women, when the vast amount of soldiering going on in the country was a cause of much trembling to the sex, there lived in a village near the Wessex coast two ladies of good report, though unfortunately of limited means. The elder was a Mrs. Martha Garland, a landscape-painter's widow, and the other was her only daughter Anne.

Anne was fair, very fair, in a poetical sense; but in complexion she was of that particular tint between blonde and brunette which is inconveniently left without a name.

A Laodicean, published in 1881, drew upon early autobio-graphical material. The hero is, in fact, an architect, and Hardy begins his first page with a description of the sun enveloping the unidentified young man and the stonework of the church he is sketching in a "lingering auriate haze," a pretty, atmospheric picture that Hardy continues throughout the chapter.

The sun blazed down and down, till it was within half-an-hour of its setting; but the sketcher still lingered at his occupation of measuring and copying the chevroned doorway—a bold and quaint example of a transitional style of architecture, which formed the tower entrance to an English village church. The graveyard being quite open on its western side, the tweed-clad figure of the young draughtsman, and the tall mass of antique masonry which rose above him to a battlemented parapet, were fired to a great brightness by the solar rays, that crossed the neighbouring mead like a warp of gold threads, in whose mazes groups of equally lustrous gnats danced and wailed incessantly.

The following year Hardy attempted a story that placed the lives of two infinitesimal beings against the Universe, an aim that went all but unnoticed in the resulting cries of immorality and sacrilege. Despite the grand design of the book, the opening sentences of *Two on a Tower* are—except for the skeleton imagery—almost mundane.

On an early winter afternoon, clear but not cold, when the vegetable world was a weird multitude of skeletons through whose ribs the sun shone freely, a gleaming landau came to a pause on the crest of a hill in Wessex. The spot was where the old Melchester Road, which the carriage had hitherto followed, was joined by a drive that led round into a park at no great distance off.

The footman alighted, and went to the occupant of the carriage, a lady about eight- or nine-and-twenty. She was looking through the opening afforded by a field-gate at the undulating stretch of country beyond. In pursuance of some remark from her the servant looked in the same direction.

By now, Hardy's intentions *were* more ambitious, and his determination to make his novels tragedies in the classical sense led to the dark stories that follow, stories that gave him a reputation for pessimism. *The Mayor of Casterbridge* begins with Something Happening—the arrival of a couple at a village and the subsequent sale of the wife by her husband on a drunken dare.

One evening of late summer, before the nineteenth century had reached one-third of its span, a young man and woman, the latter carrying a child, were approaching the large village of Weydon-Priors, in Upper Wessex, on foot. They were plainly but not ill clad, though the thick hoar of dust which had accumulated on their shoes and garments from an obviously long journey lent a disadvantageous shabbiness to their appearance just now.

The man was of fine figure, swarthy, and stern in aspect; and he showed in profile a facial angle so slightly inclined as to be almost perpendicular.

By the publication of *The Woodlanders* in 1887, Hardy was satisfied that he could hold his own as a novelist. Secure in his Wessex surroundings, he began this novel by placing it in the woodlands that would bound the story.

The Mayor of Casterbridge

by Thomas Hardy.
Author of "Far from the Madding Crowd"; "A Pair of Blue Eyes," &c.

Chapter I.

One evening of late summer, before the present century had reached its middle-age, a young man & woman, the latter carrying a child, were approaching the large village of Weydon-Priors on foot. They were plainly but not ill clad, though the thick hoar of dust which had accumulated on their shoes & clothing from an obviously long journey lent a disadvantageous shabbiness

The first page of the original manuscript of Thomas Hardy's *The Mayor of Casterbridge*. Hardy changed the beginning phrase to "before the nineteenth centruy had reached one-third of its span. . . . " *(The Trustees of the Thomas Hardy Memorial Collection in the Dorset County Museum, Dorchester, Dorset)*

The rambler who, for old association's sake, should trace the forsaken coach-road running almost in a meridional line from Bristol to the south shore of England, would find himself during the latter half of his journey in the vicinity of some extensive woodlands, interspersed with apple-orchards. Here the trees, timber or fruit-bearing as the case may be, make the wayside hedges ragged by their drip and shade, their lower limbs stretching in level repose over the road, as though reclining on the insubstantial air. At one place, on the skirts of Blackmoor Vale, where the bold brow of High-Stoy Hill is seen a mile or two ahead, the leaves lie so thick in autumn as to completely bury the track. The spot is lonely, and when the days are darkening the many gay charioteers now perished who have rolled along the way, the blistered soles that have trodden it, and the tears that have wetted it, return upon the mind of the loiterer.

No lesser personage than Robert Louis Stevenson pronounced Hardy's next book "vile," browbeating Henry James, who at first had considered *Tess of the d'Urbervilles* full of "beauty and charm," into agreeing that he had been quite wrong about it. Hardy's story of a pure woman dealt an unlucky and irredeemable hand by Fate begins innocently with the meeting of her father and a parson, who informs the drunken peasant, John Durbeyfield, of his noble lineage.

On an evening in the latter part of May a middle-aged man was walking homeward from Shaston to the village of Marlott, in the adjoining Vale of Blakemore or Blackmoor. The pair of legs that carried him were rickety, and there was a bias in his gait which inclined him somewhat to the left of a straight line. He occasionally gave a smart nod, as if in confirmation of some opinion, though he was not thinking of anything in particular. An empty egg-basket was slung upon his arm, the nap of his hat was ruffled, a patch being quite worn away at its brim where his thumb came in taking it off. Presently he was met by an elderly parson astride on a gray mare, who, as he rode, hummed a wandering tune.

"Good night t'ee," said the man with the basket.

"Good night, Sir John," said the parson.

Despite its detractors, *Tess* assured Hardy's stature as one of England's greatest novelists. In 1892, a year after its publication, Hardy finished the serialized version of *The Well-Beloved*, a pastoral novel that he had sketched out some years before. Not published in book form until 1897, after *Jude the Obscure*, it would please some of Hardy's critics that he had "returned" to his simpler, pastoral stories. It begins similarly to *Tess*.

A person who differed from the local wayfarers was climbing the steep road which leads through the sea-skirted townlet definable as the Street of Wells, and forms a pass into that Gibraltar of Wessex, the singular peninsula once an island, and still called such, that stretches out like the head of a bird into the English Channel. It is connected with the mainland by a long thin neck of pebbles "cast up by rages of the se," and unparalleled in its kind in Europe.

The pedestrian was what he looked like—a young man from London and the cities of the Continent. Nobody could see at present that his urbanism sat upon him only as a garment.

Jude the Obscure was different, from the first sentence. To many Victorian eyes, its subject matter was unspeakable; its depictions of marriage inside and outside of the law were shocking. Even by today's standards, its description of Jude and Sue's discovery of their three children hanged by the eldest is chilling. It is a grim masterpiece; bookburnings and derision made it Hardy's last.

The schoolmaster was leaving the village, and everybody seemed sorry. The miller at Cresscombe lent him the small white tilted cart and horse to carry his goods to the city of his destination, about twenty miles off, such a vehicle proving of quite sufficient size for the departing teacher's effects. For the school-house had been partly furnished by the managers, and the only cumbersome article possessed by the master, in addition to the packing-case of books, was a cottage piano that he had bought at an auction during the year in which he thought of learning instrumental music. But the enthusiasm having waned he had never acquired any skill in playing, and the purchased article had been a perpetual trouble to him ever since in moving house.

Experimenting with the novel form in the 1920s, as Hardy was approaching the end of his life, Ernest Hemingway wrote with a fortrightness that combined journalistic factuality and conciseness with conversational cadences. The result was a lean, powerful, naked style that was to influence whole generations of writers. Although it has been popular in recent years to belittle and parody Hemingway's work, the truth and the rhythm and the beauty remain, and we can marvel at the utter simplicity of great Hemingway beginnings.

Ernest Hemingway's first published novel, dissecting the dissolute lives of expatriate Americans living in Paris—as he was in 1926—was *The Sun Also Rises*. The beginning on which Hemingway finally settled after two other attempts is the description of one of the Americans by another, a newspaperman called Jake Barnes.

Robert Cohn was once middleweight boxing champion of Princeton. Do not think that I am very much impressed by that as a boxing title, but it meant a lot to Cohn. He cared nothing for boxing, in fact he disliked it, but he learned it painfully and thoroughly to counteract the feeling of inferiority and shyness he had felt on being treated as a Jew at Princeton. There was a certain inner comfort in knowing he could knock down anybody who was snooty to him, although, being very shy and a thoroughly nice boy, he never fought except in the gym.

A Farewell to Arms was Hemingway's 1929 version of his love affair with Agnes von Kurowsky, the nurse who had tended him in a Milan hospital in 1918, when he had been badly wounded in Italy. It begins with a flashback description that is poetic in its rhythm and word pictures.

> In the late summer of that year we lived in a house in a village that looked across the river and the plain to the mountains. In the bed of the river there were pebbles and boulders, dry and white in the sun, and the water was clear and swiftly moving and blue in the channels. Troops went by the house and down the road and the dust they raised powdered the leaves of the trees. The trunks of the trees too were dusty and the leaves fell early that year and we saw the troops marching along the road and the dust rising and leaves, stirred by the breeze, falling and the soldiers marching and afterward the road bare and white except for the leaves.

Although short stories intervened, Hemingway did not produce another novel until 1937, with *To Have and Have Not,* placed in Key West, where he was then living. The opening is intimately conversational, even if we do not know how it was in Cuba, as he did.

> You know how it is there early in the morning in Havana with the bums still asleep against the walls of the buildings; before even the ice wagons come by with ice for the bars? Well, we came across the square from the dock to the Pearl of San Francisco Café to get coffee and there was only one beggar awake in the square and he was getting a drink out of the fountain. But when we got inside the café and sat down, there were the three of them waiting for us.

For Whom the Bell Tolls, published in 1940, was based on his adventures in Spain during the Civil War three years earlier. It begins (and ends) in the Impersonal, with the professor hero, Robert Jordan, lying on the ground in the pine forest.

> He lay flat on the brown, pine-needled floor of the forest, his chin on his folded arms, and high overhead the wind blew in the tops of the pine trees. The mountainside sloped gently where he lay; but below it was steep and he could see the dark of the oiled road winding through the pass. There was a stream alongside the road and far down the pass he saw a mill beside the stream and the falling water of the dam, white in the summer sunlight.
> "Is that the mill?" he asked.
> "Yes."
> "I do not remember it."
> "It was built since you were here. The old mill is farther down; much below the pass."

Across the River and Into the Trees, published in 1950, allowed Hemingway to relive his war experiences and his recent trip to Northern Italy in the hero, Colonel Cantwell, who is seen as a boy wounded during the war and then as a middle-aged man returning to the same sites. This book, a best seller despite disappointing reviews, also opens in the Impersonal.

> They started two hours before daylight, and at first, it was not necessary to break the ice across the canal as other boats

had gone on ahead. In each boat, in the darkness, so you could not see, but only hear him, the poler stood in the stern, with his long oar. The shooter sat on a shooting stool fastened to the top of a box that contained his lunch and shells, and the shooter's two, or more, guns were propped against the load of the wooden decoys. Somewhere, in each boat, there was a sack with one or two live mallard hens, or a hen and a drake, and in each boat there was a dog who shifted and shivered uneasily at the sound of the wings of the ducks that passed overhead in the darkness.

All the ground that Hemingway had lost since *For Whom the Bell Tolls* was restored with the masterpiece of the sea stories, *The Old Man and the Sea.* The novelette of the old Cuban fisherman appeared in 1952, printed in its entirety in one issue of *Life* magazine, and winning a Pulitzer Prize in 1953. Two years later it helped earn him the Nobel Prize, an honor, incidentally, that had never been offered to Thomas Hardy. Like his last two novels, it, too, begins in the Impersonal.

He was an old man who fished alone in a skiff in the Gulf Stream and he had gone eighty-four days now without taking a fish. In the first forty days a boy had been with him. But after forty days without a fish the boy's parents had told him that the old man was now definitely and finally *salao,* which is the worst form of unlucky, and the boy had gone at their orders in another boat which caught three good fish the first week. It made the boy sad to see the old man come in each day with his skiff empty and he always went down to help him carry either the coiled lines or the gaff and harpoon and the sail that was furled around the mast. The sail was patched with flour sacks and, furled, it looked like the flag of permanent defeat.

Islands in the Stream, part of a trilogy of sea stories on which Hemingway had been working for years, appeared posthumously in 1970.

The house was built on the highest part of the narrow tongue of land between the harbor and the open sea. It had lasted through three hurricanes and it was built solid as a ship. It was shaded by tall coconut palms that were bent by the trade wind and on the ocean side you could walk out of the door and down the bluff across the white sand and into the Gulf Stream. The water of the Stream was usually a dark blue when you looked out at it when there was no wind. But when you walked out into it there was just the green light of the water over that floury white sand and you could see the shadow of any big fish a long time before he could ever come in close to the beach.

How has the intervening half century since Hemingway changed the style of the novel and its beginnings? Authors like Joyce Carol Oates, Kurt Vonnegut, and Martin Amis play word games with short, disjointed sentences that sometimes are meant to make sense, sometimes not. Novels begin faster, slicker, smarter. Rare today is the involved, though highly literate opening, of for example, Henry James's *The Europeans.*

A narrow graveyard in the heart of a bustling, indifferent city, seen from the windows of a gloomy-looking inn, is at no time an object of enlivening suggestion; and the spectacle is not at its best when the mouldy tombstones and funereal umbrage have received the ineffectual refreshment of a dull, moist snow-fall. If, while the air is thickened by this frosty drizzle, the calendar should happen to indicate that the blessed vernal season is already six weeks old, it will be admitted that no depressing influence is absent from the scene.

Or the slow-moving, lengthy opening of Nathaniel Hawthorne's *The Scarlet Letter.*

A throng of bearded men, in sad-colored garments, and gray, steeple-crowned hats, intermixed with women, some wearing hoods, and others bareheaded, was assembled in front of a wooden edifice, the door of which was heavily timbered with oak, and studded with iron spikes.
The founders of a new colony, whatever Utopia of human virtue and happiness they might originally project, have invariably recognized it among their earliest practical necessities to allot a portion of the virgin soil as a cemetery, and another portion as the site of a prison.

Or the convoluted beginning of Benjamin Disraeli's *Coningsby.*

It was a bright May morning some twelve years ago, when a youth of still tender age, for he had certainly not entered his teens by more than two years, was ushered into the waiting room of a house in the vicinity of St. James's Square, which, though with the general appearance of a private residence, and that too of no very ambitious character, exhibited at this period symptoms of being occupied for some public purpose.

Compare these openings with Oates's *You Must Remember This*:

Not once upon a time but a few years ago. Last year. Last week. Last Thursday. On Union Street, on Cadboro, up in the Decker project, up behind the high school in that alley. In Kilbirnie Park. Out by the reservoir. In the middle of the night, at six in the morning. In broad daylight.

Or her novel *The Assassins*:

I was born. It was born. So it began. It continues. It will outlive me. People whisper, stare, giggle. Their eternal privilege. My eternal curse. I am in a tiny place without walls. It is stifling here—but the walls are gone. No ceiling. A black hole of a ceiling. Floor? Invisible. I believe there is a floor. There must be a floor. It is invisible, like the ceiling. The walls are shoved up close, that is why the air is opaque tonight. Is it night? It has been night for some time. It is night again. Night sounds are with me always. Like the sea, the distant sea.

Or Kurt Vonnegut's *Deadeye Dick*:

> To the as-yet-unborn, to all innocent wisps of undifferenti-
> ated nothingness: Watch out for life.
>   I have caught life. I have come down with life. I was a
> wisp of undifferentiated nothingness, and then a little peep-
> hole opened quite suddenly. Light and sound poured in.
> Voices began to describe me and my surroundings. Noth-
> ing they said could be appealed. They said I was a boy
> named Rudolph Waltz, and that was that. They said the
> year was 1932, and that was that. They said I was in Mid-
> land City, Ohio, and that was that.

Generalizing is dangerous, however, especially when we
are speaking about style. Just as we conclude that the modern
novel is characterized by short, snappy beginning sentences,
a John Fowles lapses back into an Edwardian mode, or conversely, Dickens surprises us with a beginning as contemporary as Updike.

Dickens, of course, was exuberantly inventive. Mozartian
in his prodigious output, he would have had no trouble
matching, or even leading, today's literary experimentation.
No other author provides us with as many examples—
strong, entertaining examples—of the variety of beginnings
we have discussed here. It is as if, turning out stories for con-
sumption by an insatiable magazine readership, he felt
obliged to produce something different every time. His characters may be theatrical, his stories drenched in pathos and
sentiment, but his beginnings are never less than great.

In *The Posthumous Papers of the Pickwick Club,* serialized in 1836–37 when Dickens was in his twenties and still a newspaper reporter, he masquerades as the Faux-Author.

The first ray of light which illumines the gloom, and converts into a dazzling brilliancy that obscurity in which the earlier history of the public career of the immortal Pickwick would appear to be involved, is derived from the perusal of the following entry in the Transactions of the Pickwick Club, which the editor of these papers feels the highest pleasure in laying before his readers as a proof of the careful attention, indefatigable assiduity, and nice discrimination with which his search among the multifarious documents confided to him has been conducted.
"May 12, 1827. Joseph Smiggers, Esq., P.V.P.M.P.C.,* presiding. The following resolutions unanimously agreed to: *Perpetual Vice-President—Member Pickwick Club.

The darkly sinister *Oliver Twist,* in 1838, begins at the beginning. Enter the Hero.

Among other public buildings in a certain town, which for many reasons it will be prudent to refrain from mentioning, and to which I will assign no fictitious name, there is one anciently common to most towns, great or small: to wit, a workhouse; and in this workhouse was born; on a day and date which I need not trouble myself to repeat, inasmuch as it can be of no possible consequence to the reader, in this stage of the business at all events; the item of mortality whose name is prefixed to the head of this chapter.

For a long time after it was ushered into this world of
sorrow and trouble, by the parish surgeon, it remained a
matter of considerable doubt whether the child would sur-
vive to bear any name at all; in which case it is somewhat
more than probable that these memoirs would never have
appeared; or, if they had, that being comprised within a
couple of pages, they would have possessed the inestimable
merit of being the most concise and faithful specimen of
biography extant in the literature of any age or country.

Nicholas Nickleby in 1839, began with a typically Victorian-
length opening and A Little Background:

There once lived, in a sequestered part of the county of
Devonshire, one Mr. Godfrey Nickleby, a worthy gentleman, who, taking it into his head rather late in life that he
must get married, and not being young enough or rich
enough to aspire to the hand of a lady of fortune, had wedded an old flame out of mere attachment, who in her turn
had taken him for the same reason. Thus two people, who
cannot afford to play cards for money, sometimes sit down
to a quiet game for love.

Some ill-conditioned persons who sneer at the life-
matrimonial may perhaps suggest, in this place, that the good
couple would be better likened to two principals in a spar-
ring match, who, when fortune is low and backers scarce,
will chivalrously set to, for the mere pleasure of the buffeting;
and in one respect, indeed, this comparison would

hold good: for, as the adventurous pair of the Fives' Court will afterwards send round a hat, and trust to the bounty of the lookers-on for the means of regaling themselves, so Mr. Godfrey Nickleby and *his* partner, the honeymoon being over, looked out wistfully into the world, relying in no inconsiderable degree upon chance for the improvement of their means.

In *The Old Curiosity Shop* the narration is in the First Person.

Night is generally my time for walking. In the summer I often leave home early in the morning, and roam about fields and lanes all day, or even escape for days or weeks together, but saving in the country I seldom go out until after dark, though, Heaven be thanked, I love its light and feel the cheerfulness it sheds upon the earth, as much as any creature living.

I have fallen insensibly into this habit, both because it favours my infirmity and because it affords me greater opportunity of speculating on the characters and occupations of those who fill the streets.

In *Barnaby Rudge,* Dickens begins with Time:

In the year 1775, there stood upon the borders of Epping Forest, at a distance of about twelve miles from London—measuring from the Standard in Cornhill, or rather from the spot on or near to which the Standard used to be in days of yore—a house of public entertainment called the

Maypole; which fact was demonstrated to all such travellers as could neither read nor write (and sixty years ago a vast number both of travellers and stay-at-homes were in this condition) by the emblem reared on the roadside over against the house, which, if not of those goodly proportions that Maypoles were wont to present in olden times, was a fair young ash, thirty feet in height, and straight as any arrow that ever English yeoman drew.

Martin Chizzlewit, only popular on its publication for the parts that satirized America, begins with the introduction of the Chuzzlewit family:

As no lady or gentleman, with any claims to polite breeding, can possibly sympathise with the Chuzzlewit Family without being first assured of the extreme antiquity of the race, it is a great satisfaction to know that it undoubtedly descended in a direct line from Adam and Eve; and was, in the very earliest times, closely connected with the agricultural interest. If it should ever be urged by grudging and malicious persons, that a Chuzzlewit, in any period of the family history, displayed an overweening amount of family pride, surely the weakness will be considered not only pardonable but laudable, when the immense superiority of the house to the rest of mankind, in respect of this its ancient origin, is taken into account.

Dombey and Son, too, begins with the Entrance of the Heroes.

Dombey sat in the corner of the darkened room in the great armchair by the bedside, and Son lay tucked up warm in a little basket bedstead, carefully disposed on a low settee immediately in front of the fire and close to it, as if his constitution were analogous to that of a muffin, and it was essential to toast him brown while he was very new.

Dombey was about eight-and-forty years of age. Son about eight-and-forty minutes. Dombey was rather bald, rather red, and though a handsome well-made man, too stern and pompous in appearance, to be prepossessing. Son was very bald, and very red, and though (of course) an undeniably fine infant, somewhat crushed and spotty in his general effect, as yet.

In *David Copperfield,* Dickens reverted to the First Person ...

Whether I shall turn out to be the hero of my own life, or whether that station will be held by anybody else, these pages must show. To begin my life with the beginning of my life, I record that I was born (as I have been informed and believe) on a Friday, at twelve o'clock at night. It was remarked that the clock began to strike, and I began to cry, simultaneously.

... in *Bleak House,* to uncharacteristic Brevity ...

London. Michaelmas Term lately over, and the Lord Chancellor sitting in Lincoln's Inn Hall. Implacable November weather. As much mud in the streets, as if the waters had but newly retired from the face of the earth, and it would not be wonderful to meet a Megalosaurus, forty feet long or so, waddling like an elephantine lizard up Holborn Hill.

... in *Hard Times,* to the Quotation ...

"Now, what I want is, Facts. Teach these boys and girls nothing but Facts. Facts alone are wanted in life. Plant nothing else, and root out everything else. You can only form the minds of reasoning animals upon Facts; nothing else will ever be of any service to them. This is the principle on which I bring up my own children, and this is the principle on which I bring up these children. Stick to Facts, sir!"

The scene was a plain, bare, monotonous vault of a schoolroom, and the speaker's square forefinger emphasized his observations by underscoring every sentence with a line on the schoolmaster's sleeve.

... in *Little Dorrit,* to the Weather ...

Thirty years ago, Marseilles lay burning in the sun, one day. A blazing sun upon a fierce August day was no greater rarity in southern France then, than at any other time, before or since. Everything in Marseilles, and about Marseilles, had stared at the fervid sky, and been stared at in return, until a staring habit had become universal there. Strangers were stared out of countenance by staring white houses, staring white walls, staring white streets, staring tracts of arid road, staring hills from which verdure was burnt away. The only things to be seen not fixedly staring and glaring were the vines drooping under their load of grapes. These did occasionally wink a little, as the hot air barely moved their faint leaves.

… in *A Tale of Two Cities,* to the Statement of Philosophy …

It was the best of times, it was the worst of times, it was the age of wisdom, it was the age of foolishness, it was the epoch of belief, it was the epoch of incredulity, it was the season of Light, it was the season of Darkness, it was the spring of hope, it was the winter of despair, we had everything before us, we had nothing before us, we were all going direct to Heaven, we were all going direct the other way—in short, the period was so far like the present period, that some of its noisiest authorities insisted on its being received, for good or for evil, in the superlative degree of comparison only.

There were a king with a large jaw, and a queen with a plain face, on the throne of England; there were a king with a large jaw, and a queen with a fair face, on the throne of France. In both countries it was clearer than crystal to the lords of the State preserves of loaves and fishes, that things in general were settled for ever.

… in *Great Expectations,* to the First Person …

My father's family name being Pirrip, and my Christian name Philip, my infant tongue could make of both names nothing longer or more explicit than Pip. So I called myself Pip, and came to be called Pip.

I give Pirrip as my father's family name on the authority of his tombstone and my sister—Mrs. Joe Gargery, who married the blacksmith. As I never saw my father or my mother, and never saw any likeness of either of them (for their days were long before the days of photographs), my first fancies regarding what they were like were unreasonably derived from their tombstones.

… in *Our Mutual Friend,* there was Something Happening.…

In these times of ours, though concerning the exact year there is no need to be precise, a boat of dirty and disreputable appearance, with two figures in it, floated on the Thames, between Southwark Bridge which is of iron, and London Bridge which is of stone, as an autumn evening was closing in.

The figures in this boat were those of a strong man with ragged grizzled hair and a sun-browned face, and a dark girl of nineteen or twenty, sufficiently like him to be recognisable as his daughter.

Dickens's last book, *The Mystery of Edwin Drood,* written when he was ill and forcing himself to undertake a punishing schedule of public readings, was never finished. Fortunately, however, we do have his Great Beginning:

An ancient English Cathedral tower? How can the ancient English Cathedral tower be there! The well-known massive grey square tower of its old Cathedral? How can that be here! There is no spike of rusty iron in the air between the eye and it from any point of the real prospect. What is the spike that intervenes, and who has set it up?

The End ∾

Any serious writer would consider him or herself blessed to have composed even a single opening line from some of the selections in this book. That many authors were able to repeat this miracle in book after book, and then build upon those first lines to create stories and characters that live for us long after we have finished reading—some for the rest of our lives—is daunting enough to keep us from pen and paper forever. The joy of writing, however, is that there is no "right" way to write, no "right" style to use, no "right" way to begin. Ten novelists describing a mountain would describe ten different mountains. If nothing else, *Great Beginnings* is comforting proof of the fact that every writer's voice is unique, and it is the differences, not the similarities, that make a story worth beginning.

Great Beginnings. Short. Long. Descriptive. Active. Philosophic. Each of them a small gem, a mini-masterpiece, and most of all, a joyful solution to Bertie Wooster's "dashed difficult problem of where to begin."

Copyright Acknowledgments ∽

Author Index ~

Title Index〜